The Emigrants

Glynn Sinclare

Shield Crest

ISBN: 978-1-911090-78-6

MMXVII

A CIP catalogue record for this book
is available from the British Library

Published by
ShieldCrest,
Aylesbury, Buckinghamshire,
HP22 5RR   England
Tel: +44 (0) 333 8000 890
www.shieldcrest.co.uk

Dedicated to my Daddy's love of literature and Poetry
and Mammy's skills in letter writing

"It is not that I'm so smart; it is just that I stay with
problems longer"

Albert Einstein.

INTRODUCTION

Social History of the Sixties and Seventies

In the twilight of my years, I look at the successes and struggles in my life, both little and large. I realise that everything I have ever done, every person I have ever met, every experience I have had, is part of who I am today. I was born in Limerick, Ireland. I recall how it was in my childhood, the stories told by my grandmother about her life and her parents, my father and his family stories.

When I arrived in England aged seventeen I met my husband. Times were difficult; we both were emigrants from different parts of the world. I open with John's story as an introduction told by various members of his family, seen through their eyes.

I would tell little stories of my experience to my children and see a glazed look come over their eyes. Out would come their imaginary violins to play a sorrowful tune. These stories relate to how it was, in my early days. I do not hold it against them, as the life they experienced was much improved.

When I lived in Ireland, I would love to listen to my grandmother and father tell family stories of how it was during their lifetimes. I regret not having made a record of their experience or asked more questions.

I have long wanted to recount my early years as an immigrant, before my generation moved on. It was a unique time in the 60s and 70s with the movements of flower power, free love, music, creativity, poor housing and no money. We knew we were in a time of change. We were pioneers of our time, experimenting with different music, new thinking and finding new paths.

I put off writing my story until I retired and found the power to write without censure. I have painful memory of that time and I was afraid of opening Pandora's Box. I was in a hurry to start my grown-up life. I have dabbled in memories of a happy childhood.

Drink, drugs and free love were the last things on my mind. Learning to cope and surviving in an environment I did not have the emotional tools to deal with, so my everyday life was a challenge that I met face on.

Chapter 1

John's Story

In a lot of third world countries, family members who emigrated and did well for themselves, sent money home to their relatives and if the family were lucky, when they died, they would be remembered in their will. That was the way with Laura and her sisters; they were left a bequest in their brother's will. He had immigrated to America many years before; his wife would send a parcel now and then and a little money at Christmas time. There would be a hat for church and little gifts for the children. Laura had to put the bequest to good use and invest it properly. Laura had twelve children and she picked her son John as her investment. He was the most reliable. He was hard working and showed promise. She groomed him well, letting him know the trust she placed in him and the responsibility he had to the family, who would depend on him to progress. Laura's two sisters did the same; they sent a son to England in the hope and knowledge that they would help a brother or sister to improve their situation. As soon as they got to England and got a job, they would save and send the money to a brother to purchase a ticket to travel to the United States, Canada, or England for work. It did not matter where, whoever would have them and allow them to earn a living. They would work and the family would prosper. This happened in a lot of cases. There were always the ones who could not make it and fell by the wayside. When the pressure of the cold, work, loneliness and just plain inability to cope built up, they gave up. Not all could be shining lights. Some turned to drink; others their income was so low it covered the rent of a room and food. To send money home, put them in real hardship. They were some that would have to borrow money to go to work on Monday.

John had lived in Trinidad since he was four, his family having moved there from Grenada. Now as a young man, John would start his long journey to England, but first he had to return to Grenada to get his passport and get his papers in order. When that was accomplished he would take the boat from Grenada to England. Before leaving Trinidad his mother prepared him. She taught him how to cook, as he would have to look after himself in the UK. His family made great preparation for his departure and packed his brown leather suitcase. When he arrived in England and got a job, he would send money to his mother, who paid for his passage, to travel by ship to England and she financially helped him. Going to England required a suit, a very large expense, but essential. John travelled to San Fernando, to a Chinese tailor and had a dark navy blue Mohair suit made for him in two days. If he had waited until he got to England to purchase it, he would have been able to purchase two suits for the price he paid in Trinidad.

He was a very handsome Indian boy aged 20, nicely dressed, hardworking and good to his mother and younger siblings. He had a good brain and a pleasant disposition. He was born in Paraclete, Grenada on 12th July 1941 and registered in St Andrew's, Grenada, the sixth of 12 children. As he was only four when he moved with his family to Trinidad, he did not remember much about Grenada. On his return, he was told that his eldest sister Sarah was a second mother to him, she looked after him and his siblings, with the help of the mother's two sisters and his older siblings.

John's father and mother, Andrew and Laura left for Trinidad. Andrew, his father, was the first to leave Grenada and go to Trinidad, to prepare the way for the family to emigrate. He got a job in the oilfield area in Trinidad and settled into Trinidad life. Laura, his mother, did not hear from Andrew for some months, she made inquiries from Grenadians who settled in Trinidad. They could travel to where he lived, see him and report back to her. The news was not good; he had a lady living with him in his house. A family discussion ensued, Laura's sister said, "What happened to Andrew? You'd best go and sort him out."

The decision was made to leave the children with Laura's eldest daughter Sarah and siblings'. She would be under the supervision and care of the mother's sisters, her aunts. This was a very serious situation for Laura, as Andrew was the sole support of the family of seven.

Laura set off on her journey to Trinidad by boat. After disembarking, she made her way to the oilfield area. She made some inquiries of local people and found Andrew's house. Andrew was at work and true enough there was a lady in situ. Laura approached her and asked her, "What are you doing in my husband's house?" The lady said she was living with Andrew. Laura folded her arms and said, "I am his legally married wife, I have seven children with him, you have to go, there is no place for you here." The lady saw the hopelessness of her situation so she packed and left. When Andrew came back from work, Laura pointed out his responsibility to his children and wife and after showing him the error of his ways, she settled in and that was that.

After a short time Laura was expecting her eighth child. She loved her children and needed them with her in Trinidad, where they could be properly looked after, by her. She would not trust her husband to stay in Trinidad on his own while she returned to Grenada to collect her children. He may bring the other woman back into their house again, when she left.

The Family Immigrated to Trinidad

Laura sent her husband Andrew back to Grenada, to collect their children and bring them back with him to Trinidad. The seventh child born in Grenada was very small and delicate; it was thought that he would not survive the journey to Trinidad. A shroud was bought so that if the baby died on board the boat, he would be buried at sea. He was under two at the time. He survived and lived a long and healthy life.

When Andrew arrived in Grenada, he found that Sarah had settled down and married a brother of her aunt's husband. Andrew asked her to leave Grenada and travel with him and the children to Trinidad; she would not leave her husband. There was great sadness and tears when they took their leave of the family. The aunt's cousins and Sarah gathered to bid a last farewell. It was a very emotional moment. Sarah started a scene, screaming, crying and wanting them to stay. She was torn between staying with her husband and going with her father and her family. The father sent Sarah to the shop to get sweets for the children for their journey. While she was gone, the car came and they left.

Sarah was very attached to the little ones; she was a quiet softly-spoken girl. She felt she was prevented from saying goodbye to them. She was heartbroken; she had lost her family in one clear sweep and she reminisced about it towards the end of her life. She built up the story and truly believed that it was her mother, who had taken the children and not allowed her to say goodbye. It was never going to be easy. It was the custom in large families that older siblings took charge of the younger children; became substitute parents to them. Travelling to Trinidad was made easier with the help of the older children, leaving Andrew free to arrange for food and transport to the oil field area and bring them safely back to his wife Laura, to the start of their new life in Trinidad. The family settled down, the children were sent to school and their life progressed in a meaningful way.

John's Return to Grenada

Trinidad was heading towards independence in 1962 and it was decided that John would go to Grenada to get his passport as he was born there and it would be easier to go to England from Grenada, as it was a member of the Commonwealth. It was also an opportunity to get reacquainted with his sister Sarah and family in Grenada. When he arrived, he was told that Sarah was a second mother to him. There were two of his aunts, his mother's sisters, living on the same road as Sarah. His sister's husband's brother was married to one of her aunts and a third brother was married and lived on the road as well as Laura's other sisters and families. The road appeared to be owned by family. When the children grew up, they bought land, or their parents, if they could, would give them a house spot to build their house on. And so they stayed close together. Sarah had 10 children by then, she went on to have 14.

John saw large families as poverty and that stayed with him for the rest of his life. He realised they also needed financial help. Grenada may not have a lot in financial terms but families had a cow for milk, a garden for vegetables and a verity of fruit trees, a little land where they grew bananas, coco, nutmeg, plantain and citrus fruits and a husband who butchered during the week and sold meat in the market on Saturday.

They had fish from the sea, they were better off than some and well situated. All the children were healthy, everyone was fed. There was always family land and when there was plenty, it was always shared. That did not mean they did not work. The land had to be cultivated, grass had to be cut and the cow had to be fed before and after school. All the family had work to do and each one knew their task. If they neglected or forgot to do it, they got a sharp reminder. There was a hive of activity when it was time to butcher at the weekend.

Some of their land was far away, on the mountain near Grand Etang Lake. The earth was rich and black, nutmeg trees grew there. This meant a long journey by transport or donkey, walking up the steep hill to work the land and pick the nutmeg. Married daughters spent days with their mother, helping her with the chores; they were rewarded with what was plentiful to take back to their homes, some fruit and vegetables, fish or meat, to cook for their husbands on their return from work.

John learned when he got to Grenada that two cousins were preparing to leave for England around the time he was due to travel. One cousin on his mother's side was going to join her fiancé; she was waiting for him to send her ticket. She would get married in England. A cousin named Rita, on his father's side was going to study nursing ... There were already some cousins and uncles in England and they would help John to settle when he arrived. He spent the next few weeks getting his passport in Grenada. It came as a shock to him to find out that his first name differed on his birth certificate and the spelling of his surname was missing one letter which changed the sound of his name. It was not unusual to register the birth of a child with one christening name and call the child by another, a home name. Also the person who registered the birth was not always the parent; it could have been a family member. They would make a guess at the spelling of the name, or the registrar would make a guess. There are three different spellings of his surname in his family.

John paid a visit to all his relatives in Grenada, on his mother's instructions. He first went to pay his respects to his grandmother whose name was Louise but she was referred to as Ms John, her late husband's first name was John. Ms John was a strong lady. Her granddaughter recounts a story about her death.

Rita had sent her a beautiful pink nightie. She was nearing her last hours and it was decided that she should wear the item to greet her Maker. Ms John got out of bed with the help of her stick ranting and raving for her old nightie. It was retrieved, washed and when dried Ms John donned her nightie, lay on her bed and passed peacefully away. She was over 100 years old. The local school and church rang their bells in her honour; she had been the oldest lady in the district.

John met his cousin Rita who was travelling to England to do nursing. She was a very beautiful girl and she was ready to travel. She asked John to travel at the same time as her and they would look out for one another. She was in love with a boy who was immigrating to America. Her mother did not like him. She felt that it would prevent her daughter from perusing her studies and stop her from becoming a nurse. She banned her daughter from keeping company with him and kept her on a short leash. Her mother was a hard working widow who had educated her two daughters. There was a farewell party for Rita, the night before she left; she managed to get away with her friend. Rita was very much in love; one assumes that they walked hand in hand in the moonlight along the beach listening to the sea rolling over the silver sand. Their hearts must have been breaking with the thought of their imminent separation. Many tears would have been shed and they would have found comfort in their love. She left for England with John and her boyfriend left for America. When she eventually traced him, time had passed and he was settled in America with another woman.

John Journeys to England

John and Rita left Grenada on 19 March 1961 on the ship *Irpino* travelling to England they sailed away to the many tears of relatives, made promises not to forget them, they would send a letter to let them know how they were getting on and a little money when they could. Relatives waved frantically from the docks seeing their family disappearing into the distance, not knowing if they would ever see them again. John was very sick for three days. The journey took 12 days, all they could see was sea and sky.

On board the ship, his cabin had 10 bunks and he made a note of the number of the cabin 725. The ship was 500 ft long and had 1,200 passengers on board. Every day he would walk around the ship several times thinking of where he would live and what kind of work he would get, making plans for the future... He was sure he would get work as he heard there was some to be had. He was taught in school to read by the English reader, English history and geography. When there was a royal visit or the Queen's birthday children had a day off school, lining the route with other schoolchildren and waving the British flag in the visitor's honour. England was his mother country. He was coming to the Mother Land and would be sure of a welcome.

Rita did not travel well, she was constantly sick. She rarely ventured out and stayed with the single girls in their cabin. When she did go out it was to meet John. He saw her every day for a short time. The ship arrived at Southampton Docks on the 10th April 1961, Easter Sunday. There was a surge of passengers to the side of the boat to see the dock and England for the first time. They stood shivering in the cold; their clothes inappropriate for the cold wind. Their first look was not inspiring, all seemed dark and dismal. There were no dockers working as it was a bank holiday. They had to wait until the next day for the dockers to unload the cargo so they could then disembark and get trains, buses and other transport to their final destinations. The passengers were given a sandwich, provided by the ship, at the train station to sustain them on the final train journey.

Rita was going to a different part of London, to start her nursing course. She was being met at Victoria Station by a representative from the hospital, holding a plaque with the hospital name on it. John was not sure how he would recognise the person who would be there to greet him. The platform was crowded with people meeting and greeting their friends and relatives. There was laughter and tears of relief.

Two men approached and asked him if his name was John. It was not the first young man they had stopped and asked. John had never met these men before, he had seen a photograph of his cousin at his aunt's house but he would not have been able to recognise him by that. They introduced themselves, one was a first cousin and his name was Roland. He was short, dark with a slim frame and a scarcity of hair. He was one of John's aunty's sons from Grenada. The second man's name was Len. He was also from Grenada, tall with a fair complexion born of mixed parentage, very confident about his knowledge of London. After some polite conversation about Ronald's sisters, his Ma and the neighbours, they continued to a house in Connaught Road, Harlesden.

They arrived to be greeted by more family members coming out of every room. He was offered a meal and shown to his room, which he would share with a young man called Salim. Salim was John's height, fair skinned, good looking, presentable and from a good family and he was easy to talk to. John and Salim became firm friends. John produced the bottle of rum and distributed the gifts he brought with him for the family, Guava cheese which is a sweet and black cake, baked by the aunts. The music was the latest calypso John had brought from Trinidad.

The gramophone was the first essential purchase the family made when they came to England. They could sleep to the music of the Caribbean and dream they were at home once more, with a warm breeze and the sound of the waves moving over the silver sands. A small tumbler of rum was passed around; everyone had one shot to keep out the cold. That is all it took for a party to start. The music played, the cousins cooked and danced to the music of the Caribbean. There was talk of Grenada's politics by uncles: what the politicians were not doing for Grenada, stories about who did what when they were in the

Caribbean, friends and family, inquiries about young women left behind. "Is Diana still single? Has she got anyone?" People drifted in to see John and welcome him with a nod and "When did you arrive?" There was advice from uncles who said, "Salim will go with you to get your National Insurance number, show you how to get work and show you around until you find your way about." For a short while they forgot the hardships of poor living conditions: Paraffin fires, outside toilet, cold draughts blowing in through the doors and window frames, not enough blankets on the bed, noticeboards, when looking for a room, no blacks need apply, waiting for buses in the snow and cold, the longing for hot sun, sea and sand, family and home.

Finding work

On the Monday Salim went with John to an interview at Lesme chocolate factory, he got the job and started on the Tuesday. The pay was £8.15.00 per week, a little more for shift work. This he converted into 42 Trinidad and Tobago dollars, not a lot but it had overtime and John was not afraid of hard work. John went to work at the chocolate factory roasting cocoa beans; it was an automated factory. He operated a control panel to roast cocoa beans. When the beans were roasted they were dropped by machine to another floor, to continue the melting process and they ended as slabs of chocolate. He worked two shifts, one week Monday to Saturday 7am to 7pm, six days a week. Then second week 7pm to 7am, six nights.

Rita studied nursing and qualified. She went on to pursue a successful career. John was a man who loved his family; they were his life. He was quick to help financially those who were less well-off than himself. He never missed work, even if he was ill. He would say to himself *I am not sick* and head out the door to work. He saw no shadow in his life. It was right or wrong, black or white.

Chapter 2

Marie's Story

Finding work in the 60s

Friday morning I asked Mammy for the money for the dance at the Stella and she said, "Where do you think I would get the money from?" The Stella Saturday night was the highlight of the week. In the 60s neighbours received parcels from relatives in America, with not always appropriate clothing for their children. That is how I acquired a beautiful dress and three net waist slips of pink and white. I was in my element. Now the problem was to get half a crown from Mammy to go to the dance at the Stella on Saturday night. This was no mean feat as Mammy had many calls upon her purse. After doing chores, window cleaning and dishes washed, I was given permission to go to the dance. Being on my best behaviour was not an easy thing for me to do. Bus fare or the money for a cola was out of the question. Sometimes I did not have to ask for the money to go to the dance as I worked in Woolworth's on a Saturday, Christmas and Easter holidays.

I washed my hair and put in rollers. I donned my slips and pulled over a beautiful dress of pink cotton. My makeup was Mammy's Ponds face cream, a powder puff and a faint dash of Mammy's red lipstick lightly applied so that no-one knew I had any on, rollers out and hair brushed into a pony tail. My beautiful dress stood out like a ballerina and Cuban-heeled shoes which were in fashion at the time, I felt good.

Mammy gave me the money and her last words were, if the dance finishes at 12pm be home by 12.45 pm. That was time to get my coat from the cloakroom and walk home with my brother. He and I had an arrangement to meet at the bottom of our road. Whoever came first waited, I would see him under the street light, his face glowing as he took a puff of a cigarette. We would walk home together.

Off I went down the road and in the Ennis road over the bridge and there I was at the Stella in no time. The excitement grew as I paid and entered another world. I took a step into the ballroom to see a stage filled with musicians, seven or eight, smartly dressed in coloured blazers and slacks. The girl singer was beautifully attired in a stunning dress. The Billy Conway Show band or one of the visiting show bands performed at the Stella. There were two to three brass instruments, guitars and drums, singers comparable to Elvis Presley, The Everly Brothers, Tommy Steele, Buddy Holly, girls who sang like Helen Shapiro and many others. The singers always looked so handsome when they crooned the latest hits and the girls had beautiful dresses. It was our introduction to the performing art, of live music, of a very high quality.

The dance floor was well lit, highly polished; it lent itself to rock 'n' roll, you could literally skate across the floor. There was a giant silver ball reflecting light and revolving in the centre of the ceiling. Teenagers were everywhere'; it was a kaleidoscope of colour and rock 'n' roll music. There were boys dressed in suits, Teddy boys and girls of all shapes and sizes with their hair styles of pony tails, French rolls, bouffant back combed, all looking their best.

I made my way to the cloakroom to hand in my coat, check that all was well with my appearance and to connect with my friends when they arrived. We stood in the softly-lit area under the upstairs balcony admiring one another's outfit and going over the latest gossip. In the softer lighting, you were not embarrassed, if you were not asked up for a dance or you had to refuse someone. I was sure that I danced every dance. I loved music and dancing. Every week a new hit would be released. It was a revolution in music from the classical to rock 'n' roll. Jazz and blues had always been there and were a favourite with me, so I took to rock 'n' roll like a duck to water.

Sometimes the spotlight would pick a couple dancing and they would win the spot prize. As luck would have it I won with my dance partner on more than one occasion. The prize was 10 shillings each. That was an opening for your dance partner to ask you if you would like refreshments and get to know you a little better. There was an ice cream parlour in the American style. We made our way towards the ice cream parlour to find a booth of red leather. The bar was of a transparent, iridescent light, colours of the rainbow intersected with silver bars not unlike the well-polished bumper of a 1950 American car. We were both riding high after our win. He would be very courteous and do his best to create a good impression. If he played his cards right, he may be able to walk me to the bottom of my road.

The waitress came to serve us dressed in her little black dress, with her snowy white apron, heart-shaped with lace gathered around the border, order pad in hand. Ice cream and jelly for me, a glass of Cola for him, they arrived in frosted glasses, no alcohol was served. The hall was closed at 10pm, so that men from the pub would not be let in after pub closing time. Light conversation followed: what school did he go to, or did he work, where did he live and what did his father do. Mothers were housewives, homemakers; they did not go out to work. A lot of information could be gleaned so that when the evening came to an end I could decide, whether he could walk me to the bottom of our road or I would say, I was not allowed to go home with a boy, my brother was seeing me home. I was now a teenager.

When I was younger I played on the road, Chris my brother was a year and ten months younger than me, we were close but not too close as the boys had their sports and girls had their friends and games. Chris went to the park every day to meet his friends. They played games of hurling, rugby and football. Chris went to school at the Christian Brothers School. Across the road from the Salesian Convent was the Christian Brothers woods. When the day was a clear, bright autumn day, it was an artist's pallete of colours, leaves of orange to yellow, brown, red and gold. From school we made our way up the hill towards the Union cross kicking the vast mounds of leaves. I took great pleasure in collecting one or two of the most beautiful leaves, to press in one of my school books. Up our road we went to see boys and girls, my brother Chris among them, standing or bending down, near the pavement. They were huddled in groups conferring about the hoard of marbles they recently acquired. They were in beautiful coloured patterns, green and red: multicoloured marble treasures. The competition was fierce as they took turns rolling marble, trying to hit their opponent's

12

marble to win and increase their hoard. I joined in and found I had a talent for winning marbles. I would win little by little moving down the road with the boys. When I won a little pile I would go indoors and hide them in a tin cigarette box under the mattress. This seemed to be a good idea until on one of my return visits, I came back to find my brother helping himself to my hoard. We argued and Mammy intervened, she took the box and threw the marbles out of the window into the garden. I went out in a sulk to join the girls. I searched for days after to see if there were any marbles in the garden, it never occurred to me that they had been found by Chris. They went back on the street to be lost and won many times over.

There were many activities on the road as there were many children; all the mothers seemed to be around the same age, so there were always children around our age. No matter what age my sisters and brothers were, we could always find companions to play with. Children always appeared home in time for meals, it seemed like they had a built-in clock. Spin the top was a favourite game; we watched the top racing around at high speed all eyes mesmerised by the spinning of the top, then it lost control wobbled and stopped, only to be whipped up again and again. Chris and the boys would have bicycle wheels and a stick and race down the road hitting the wheel keeping it under control, then trying to keep up with it, again sometimes if they were very lucky there was a tyre on the wheel but that was a rare occurrence. It was a great sport but mainly for the boys. The girls would be outside No 6 with skipping ropes, two girls turning the rope and the rest queuing up to run in and skip. I wish I could remember the songs. One of the rhymes for skipping was 'Skip to my Lou'. Also there was throwing the ball up against the wall to rhymes: it could have been where our love for poetry started together with nursery rhymes

As Chris got older we had discussions about girls, me telling him, "Girls like a boy with good manners." Chris had his own friends. He would go to the pool hall and play pool. We were meant to come home together. He could be seen waiting under the lamp light at the bottom of our road. His face would light up in the darkness as he puffed his cigarette, we would walk up our road together. He was slim, tall with auburn hair. A handsome boy in his teens. I would talk to him about girls, about being polite: "Stand up when a girl comes to the table or leaves the table at the coffee shop." Years later his wife said she fell for him because he had such beautiful manners.

The latest gossip at the dance was that a girl went home with a boy she did not know and when they stopped under the lamp light for a good night kiss, she looked down at his feet, they were cloven hoofed she went home with the Devil himself. We did not believe it and said the priest put that rumour out. However we were not going home with a stranger that was out of the question for a while.

For forty days of Lent all dance halls were closed down. We went to the boat club, where there was a little dancing after ballroom dance lessons. We soon gave that up as there was no comparison, to Saturday night at the Stella.

I was on school holidays and I was not one to hang about. The idea of not going to the Stella on Saturday night would be the end of my life as I knew it. So I said I would look for a job at Shannon industrial estate. It was a new estate opened at the time and there was plenty of work but very low wages. I would have to travel thirteen and a half miles by bus. Mammy agreed and gave me the bus fare,

I headed off very hopeful; it was a new adventure for me. I enjoyed the bus ride to Shannon as I always did. I heard talk on the road of the best factories SPS and Shannon Diamond. I thought I would give SPS a try. The bus stopped at Shannon Industrial Estate and I asked where SPS was. I had to walk past several factories to get to it.

I reached it and asked the receptionist, "Do you have any vacancies?" I was shown to the personnel office, given a form to fill in and then given a series of IQ tests. When I'd finished, the lady came back and interviewed me. She said, "Marie, you have done well in your tests." She was about to give me the job when she noticed I was under 18. The company policy was not to employ teenagers under that age.. She said, "I am very sorry but I cannot employ you. Come back when you are over 18."

I left undaunted as there were many other factories. I stopped at one called Lana Knit. I thought that was good. I would try there as I could knit. I went in and got the job. The wages were £2. 10 shillings per week from eight in the morning to five in the evening. I would be home by six o' clock. I would take the bus at seven in the morning at the Union Cross.

The bus fare was ten shillings and sixpence and would be deducted from my pay. (To translate shillings and pence into decimals in the pound does not relate so well ,as one has to take into account the economy and the cost of living in the sixties ...It is still very poor wages.)

My first day at work was exciting and new to me. I was shown how to do invisible mending on machine-knitted garments. I picked it up quickly as I liked to knit and embroider. I would walk around during my break and chat to people. There was a very nice girl, older than me who worked on the machines. She would put cleaning fluid on a cloth and sniff the cloth. I think she was addicted. I talked to a good looking boy working on a knitting machine He had dark, curly hair and blue eyes. He was quiet and a little shy. I asked him how old he was. He was my age and his name was Ted. I met him years later when he became a family friend of my sister. By then he was a retired company director so he successfully moved on from his year's work at Lana Knit and advanced in his career. We have met on many occasions since those early years and we journey back in memory to our time at Lana Knit, on the occasions when I visited Limerick.

In the factory there were long machines that would knit collars for cardigans at night; the machines would run with the night shift. If the men were neglectful a stitch would slip, if the needle in the machine was not replaced immediately, it would leave a run in the collar and there was a mountain of collars against a wall. I invisibly mended a few and showed them to the foreman and said to him that if we got a bonus we could mend them. He told me to go and ask the owner, who was sitting in his office. Until then I did not know he existed. I went in and showed him what I had done and said there was a mountain of collars against the wall. We could mend them. He said to show him so we went to where they were. He asked me how much I wanted. I said "nine pence a dozen" and he agreed. I do not know how I calculated that amount. It was the right amount, not too much or too little. I had not thought how much beforehand.

I knew how long it took me to do one, somewhere in my brain. I worked it out and that was good. He agreed so I was given a note book. I had to record the work done in dozens that I did myself and check the other three girls' work and enter it in the note book. I remember getting £5.17.6 in my pay. I was in my element. There was a problem with Mammy who said that when she worked before she got married she brought her pay packet home to her Mammy unopened. I gave her £5. I dug my heels in, for the balance. I enjoyed the work and accepted life as it was. I had my eye on the upcoming summer holiday to go to England, to visit my sister Phillis, who I am sure in hindsight did not want me anywhere near her. I had not told my Mammy I was not coming back. I was 17 and ready to start the rest of my life.

Chapter 3

Galway Bay

Bank holiday Monday was a special day; we would go to Galway Bay for the day. We would all trundle in to town, to the train station and on to the train, vacating our home: Mammy, Daddy, the children, my uncle, aunt and cousin.

Mammy never got the correct number of tickets, so many little ones. We boarded the train and as we all moved around, it was hard to track us. We would be standing, our heads hanging out the train window, the steam bellowing from the engine, small dots of black soot resting on our noses, while we chugged past fields of cattle and bales of hay in fields of wheat. We would investigate the other carriages to see if we knew anyone else travelling. It was hard on the inspector of the train, keeping track of us all and trying to make the tickets match the number of children on the train. We always said, "My Mammy has the tickets" or we would lock ourselves in the bathroom avoiding him completely.

This time my friends were going as well and they were staying the night in Galway. My friend Hannah's brother had a caravan, parked on a caravan site on the Galway cliff.

There were many discussions, about me staying the night, going to the dance and sleeping in the caravan with them. I had secretly given my dress and under slips to wear to the dance, to my friends to bring to Galway for me. I had not asked Mammy for permission as she would say no. So when all three of us went to her carriage on the train, together, I let Sorcha and Hannah plead with her saying "Hello, Mrs G." Mammy said, "Hello girls." Sorcha said, "Can Marie stay the night with us in Galway, we will come back on the train tomorrow. Hanna's older brother has a caravan and he promised to let us stay the night there. He will sleep in the car, he will look after us Mrs G." Mammy was in good form and with my aunt smiling at us, after much pleading she agreed. We arrived safely, said our farewells to Mammy and made our way to the caravan.

Her brother let us use the caravan and left without saying a word. We had something to eat and laid our clothes out for the dance that night. We headed towards the beach, with great excitement, chatting about the dance that night and what show band was performing. The day was very hot. The sun glistened in the cloudless sky making the sea sparkling blue green, while the sand burned hot under our feet. We decided to leave the beach. We promenaded up and down, it seemed to us that all were happy under the blue skies and sunshine, we checked out the styles Galway teenagers wore, to make sure we were trendy enough.

We avoided my family, as Mammy may ask too many questions about our sleeping arrangements. When we had enough of walking, we headed back, to get ready for the dance. It was very exciting sharing make up, asking one another "Does my hair look right? How is my dress?" Eventually we were ready to go. There was a famous show band playing that night in Galway. The bank holiday weekend was the racing weekend; there were a lot of visitors in Galway. The dance finished off the weekend to perfection. To go there would be fantastic. The singers and the band would be spectacular, we would have a ball. We headed off along the cliff road with our wide skirts and net under skirts looking stunning, one girl fair, one dark and one red head, full of glorious expectations.

The dance was the great success. We danced every dance; we met some nice Galway boys who offered to walk us along the road to the cliffs where our caravan was. We laughed and joked along the road as only young people can. Adrenaline was coursing in our veins and we did not feel the cold or we were not tired. It must have been two in the morning, as the dance finished at one. We made sure to let the boys know that they could not come all the way to the caravan site with us, as Hannah's brother would be waiting up for us and he would kill her. They were gentlemen and saw us a little way along the road.

We got back to the caravan, knocked on the door and Hannah's brother, who we woke up from his sleep, opened up and said, "You will have to sleep in the car." Hannah protested to no avail. He had friends sharing the caravan with him and they were asleep. I must have been very innocent. I thought all the arrangements were made for us to sleep in the caravan. The girls were holding back.

We settled in the car on one of the coldest nights I have ever experienced. We put on our trousers leaving on our party frocks, any other clothes we bought with us, we put on. We were given a few thin blankets to cover us. We tried to sleep, we dosed off and on through the night and at six thirty Hannah's brother felt sorry for us and took us for tea to a transport cafe in Galway. Only then did we start to warm up and come alive again. When we returned to the caravan no-one was there. We checked how much money we had between us, which was very little. We were able to buy a packet of dried vegetable soup and bread and butter and that was our lunch. We took our leave of Galway and headed back home.

On the following Sunday morning I was getting ready for early Mass, when my Daddy who was having a lie in, called me into his bedroom and said, "Marie, I want a word with you. one of my apprentices and his friend were touring around the Galway coast from the cliffs of Moher, when his car broke down and they had to spend the night in a car park on the caravan site. He said he'd seen you with two other girls sleeping in a car on one of the coldest nights in years. I said, "It wasn't me."

Chapter 4

The River Shannon

I always liked solitude, it was difficult to find peace and quiet when I was a child, as we had a large family and a full house. When I was in a solitary mood and all the children were playing on the street; which was what all children on our road did if the weather was good and it was not raining heavily, I would head off for a walk. A Soft Irish mist did not count as rain.

I would go towards the river Shannon passing the Salesian convent and turn in the direction of Barrington's Pier. I loved to be by myself, to dwell in my own thoughts. To wander in imaginings of the possibility of greatness and brilliance, only to recognise the fact, that I did not know how to achieve it. I was safe in the knowledge that I could go home when I wished.

The sight of water, rivers or sea is soothing. Since after the ice age; rivers have always flowed cascading from mountain tops, picking up heavy rainfall, winding their way through towns and villages on their journey to the sea. Since the beginning of time, its consistent flow reassures us of the continuity of life.

I would think about how many generations walked this same route along the bank of the Shannon, I wondered what their lives were like, in what way they differed from me. Was it just clothes and a lack of modern equipment?

My grandparents and great-grandparents walk this path. On a summer's evening they would enjoy the peace and serenity of the closing of the day. Sometimes I would pass neighbours walking their dogs but often at that time of day, it was quiet. Mammy's were busy at home and Daddy's were working.

Depending on my mood on other occasions, I would walk towards town, passing Cleves factory and down towards the Wellesley bridge and Arthur's Que. I would sit on an iron post, which was one of many protruding out of the ground linked with iron chains as a precaution against driving one's car into the river Shannon.

I looked down towards King John's castle and the river racing at high tides coming from Shannon Pot in the north of Ireland through Loch Allen, Loch Ree and Loch Derg making its way, passing Limerick city and out the Shannon estuary towards the sea. And at low tide, water racing over rocks and pebbles, in the white surf.

I would think of all the past generations of my family that had sat or walked along this path. I would sit and daydream about the past and my future. When would my grown-up life begin? Near tea-time, I would make my way homewards. I was never asked by Mammy "where have you been all afternoon?" It was assumed I was playing on the road. I never said.

While I am talking about Mammy, I will tell you a little story about her and the demise of the duck. One Saturday Daddy arrived with a surprise – a live duck – and said it was a gift from a farmer's wife he did a job for. Daddy was an electrician. The duck was ensconced in our back yard. Our duck was the pet of the yard, younger sisters ran and chased it, it was fed choice bits. Mammy was seen looking kindly on it with all notion of him becoming next Sunday's dinner initially dispensed with.

On Saturday afternoon I followed Mammy out to the back yard, she was carrying a spoon and a small bottle of baby Powers whiskey. She handed me the whiskey and spoon and told me, "Marie, pour the whiskey on to the spoon." I watched in amazement as she wrestled with the duck, gripping him under her arm, while she prised open his beak and asked me to administer a spoon of whiskey. My hands were shaking, there was spillage, but I administer a second spoonful. Mammy let go of the duck and he waddled off none the worse for his experience, though a little unsteadily. Mammy said that would tenderise his meat for Sunday. She was not giving up on Sunday dinner.

On Saturday Mammy and Daddy went out for a few hours. Mammy instructed me to "let Mr Keogh into the back yard to prepare the duck for Sunday lunch." He was the man who collected the kitchen waste to feed his pigs. He arrived and I let him into the yard. I closed the kitchen door and pressed my ear nervously up against it. I listened to the protest of our duck, as he departed to his happy hunting grounds. It was over in a flash. Mr Keogh called out, "I've finished." I did not open the door or look to see the deadly deed that had been carried out in our back yard. Sunday came and after Mass we were all seated around the table. Mammy brought in the duck, golden brown sitting on a plate; she placed it on the table and sat down. My little sister said, "Is that our duck? I am not eating him." Mammy was poised, knife in hand and looked at her next child who stared back at her and viewed her as the judge, who had sent our duck to the chief executioner. "I will not eat our duck," she said, One after another we all refused. Mammy then put a slice of duck on her plate while all eyes were on her. She tried to eat it but couldn't. Then, she announced, "That duck is so tough, it is no wonder that the farmer's wife gave it away, before it died from old age." We were all happy that justice had been served. I am sure Mammy gave the duck the whiskey so he would be anaesthetised when he met his untimely demise.

Chapter 5

Scarlet Fever

Mammy was busy preparing the breakfast in the kitchen. She told me to wake up my brother Chris, because if he didn't get a move on, he would be late for school. I went into his room and saw he did not look too good. He had a sore throat and a high temperature. I told Mammy and she dried her hands on the tea towel and went to see him. She looked at his throat and said he had scarlet fever. I was sent to the City Home Hospital to tell them to send an ambulance and to let them know that he had white spots in his throat. I was amazed at my Mammy's knowledge and diagnosis. A doctor was never called to our house; it was not as if we did not have all the childhood illnesses. I once heard Mammy say. 'If one of the children got sick with one of the childhood illnesses. I did not separate them as it was better to get it all over and done with at the same time.'

Her diagnosis was correct. I remember the ambulance men joking with my brother to keep him cheerful as they took him away. I am sure that Mammy was very worried. She consoled herself with the words, "He will be in the best place. He will be well looked after."

I had to go to school and hoped to be quite popular with my news when I told my classmates. It wasn't every day that someone had a brother with scarlet fever. I had recently seen a film about a mother and father dying from diphtheria and typhoid, caught when they nursed their children to good health. It was called *The Day They Gave Babies Away*. I cried with my friend all the way through. With my vivid imagination I merged diphtheria, typhoid and scarlet fever into one and visualised all the way to school that when I came home I would see a red flag waving in the wind outside our gate. Our family would be in quarantine and I wouldn't have to go to school. I was very disappointed when I had to go back to school after dinner. There were no privileges attached to my brother's illness.

There was great discussion about where and how he got scarlet fever. I had my own opinion. We would sometimes get a shilling from Daddy for the pictures. He was an electrician for the E.S.B and he had to work in the country for some time bringing electricity to the rural areas. He worked long hours away from home. We got our shilling pocket money when he was back at the weekend. He was a little more flush with money with the overtime and we were happy to be off to the cinema.

There were seats for eight pence and one shilling. Mammy wanted us to go in the one shilling seats as they were better and she thought we would be safer. The eight pence seats were near the screen I would see Chris in the eight pence seats smoking a cigarette when he inhaled; it lit up his face like a beacon. There was a little shop near the park where they sold single cigarettes he could get two for four pence. Mammy did not know he smoked. He was quite young at the time.

Mammy would tell me to run up to the city home and cheer Chris up as he would be bored. I would go and see him. They allowed me to stand in the grounds and call to my brother. He would come to an upstairs window and look out. I was not allowed to go to the ward as there are restrictions on children visitors. Our topic of conversation was about what he'd had for dinner and did he have dessert. He also had orange juice. I thought the hospital was a very fine place to be; a holiday for him.

Chapter 6

Leaving Home

It crossed my mind that I had tried to leave home before, always anxious to start my life as a grown-up.

Once again I was in trouble with Mammy. It could be a number of things; I had not figured there was more than one way, of getting my own way. On Saturday she went to the market and my sister Phillis and I had to clean out the house. Phillis had to wash and polish the dining room hall and kitchen. I thought she had the better deal as she would throw soapy water over the floor, sweep it out through the kitchen and out the back yard into the drain, dry the floor with a cloth and polish it. She would call the boys to put Daddy's old socks on, or put old woollen jumpers, on the floor. Then they would skate up and down giving it a brilliant shine and the job was done.

My job, I felt, was more difficult. I had to clean the three bedrooms, dress the beds, sweep the rooms, polish the wardrobe and dressing table. I would finish two rooms and when I got to the boys' bedroom and dressed the bed. I would pull out the bed from the wall to sweep the room, I would find comics. These were no ordinary comics; they were classic comics in colour. A family on the road got them in a parcel from America; magical things came in parcels from America. Unfortunately we did not have any relatives there to send us parcels but the brothers would swap them for marbles or some such item and so the comics would go to every house with children on our road. There were stories of the *Bible*, the *Three Musketeers*, *Jane Eyre*, *Lorna Doone* and many others.

I would lie across the bed and start reading. Time flew by and I would hear the call: Mammy is back. I would scurry about finishing off the room. Mammy would come into the bedroom, after seeing the brilliantly shining dining-room floor slightly waterlogged. She would start in full flow at my poor performance. She would get the brush and pan, go in to every nook and cranny, up the chimney if necessary, to show me the error of my ways.

This time I could not remember what it was I had done or not done. I remember being at the ironing board, ironing clothes and my Mammy's voice droning on in the background, fading away as she passed in and out of the kitchen. I announced I was leaving home. I stormed into my bedroom to get my school case. I put it on a chair next to the ironing board and started to iron my clothes from a drawer into the case, in between finishing the bundle of clothes for Mammy. When I finished I got my coat and headed for the door, up our steps and down the road. There was an absence of Mammy saying come back here, though I knew she was looking out the window. I got as far as the shop, four houses down and I realised, I had nowhere to go, so I went down the side passage of the shop and came out at the back of Riley's house. I stood under the leafy branches of the tree with my case on the ground for what seemed an eternity. It was a very grey day and it started to rain, that soft Irish rain like mist.

If I said I heard voices now they would lock me up. I have not been locked up yet. There were only four times in my life when I had these messages from somewhere else. They stopped when I left home. A voice told me three things:

One: That one day I would have a cinema in every room in my house
 Two: I would not lose my teeth, I would have china teeth over them
Three: What I gained in life I would work for

These things came to pass. I have a television or computer in every room, I have had caps on my teeth and I have worked all my life.

Time passed and my built-in clock was telling me it was around tea-time.

I was embarrassed to go home and see Mammy knowingly smile but I had no other choice. I picked up my case and headed home. As I came in through the front door to the hall, I slipped my case into my bedroom and went into the dining-room. They were all seated at the table unaware I had left home. I took my place at table. My Mammy was in and out from the kitchen laying the table. Not a word was said. I was so grateful that she did not mention it. I never unpacked my case; my Mammy must have, as everything was back in its place. That night my Mammy came in to my bedroom, to tuck in the blankets, as she always did on cold nights or if she and I had words, that is if she had words and I was not required to answer. I pretended I was asleep but I was glad.

I made my way to Pery house to bid farewell to my aunts. They kissed me, wished me well and told me to take care of myself in England. I went across to the People's park in Pery Square. As I entered the park the sun was shining on the beds of flowers, well kept, with neat borders, their colours like multi-coloured flags on display. I heard a clear voice in my head.. "This is the last time you will walk in this park as a citizen of this country." I knew there was truth in these words; the enormity of them did not strike me until years later. I hold these words in my memory. I walked around bidding farewell to the beauty of the park: its pathways where Aunty Monica walked her little dog, its bandstand, the pagoda where my Aunt Maggie sat. I gathered these memories to save them, to hold them close and keep as a blessing for the day of remembrance.

That night, I wanted to go into town to bid farewell to my friends. I had spent very pleasurable times with them: The dances at the Stella; swimming at Corbally; coffee in the Capri coffee shop. Mammy seemed upset that I was thinking of going to town. She said Daddy and herself would take me out. We went to a hotel bar. I had orange juice; girls of my age did not drink alcohol. I gave Daddy the money to buy a round and I thought myself very grown up.

The next day Mammy and sisters bid me farewell at the station. I was wearing a white pleated skirt and a thin mauve jumper. The white skirt inappropriate for travel but it looked good.

At the train station Mammy was getting agitated as there was no sign of Daddy. She was afraid he would not be there to wish me goodbye. At the last moment he came rushing into the train station. He pulled a watch out of his jacket pocket and gave it to me. It was beautiful. He showed me the second face with a second hand, so that, if I wanted to do nursing, I could use it. I was delighted as I had never had a watch before, or any jewellery come to that. I felt very important with a watch. There were tears in Mammy's eyes. I have to confess, all I felt was adventure and a sense of excitement. I had never been away from home before. Mammy used to say I was hard and had no sensitivity, but that was not true. I worried about everything long after people cried and let it go.

The train drew slowly away and I watched my family growing smaller in size, diminishing into the distance. I got a seat and looked around. There was a newly married couple not much older than me reading comics. I was horrified at the thought they were married and wanted to read comics.

My Mammy had instructed me about travel. She said when the train reached the station to call a porter and keep some change in my pocket as a tip. When I got off the boat it was the dawning of the morning. I stuck my head out of the window and waved to a porter. He took my small brown case and I walked alongside him. He asked me how my journey had been and I answered. He said I was from South Wales but I insisted no. I came from Limerick. He kept saying South Wales. He was a kind man and brought me and my case to my seat. I gave him his tip. I look back now and think, what was Mammy thinking? I had just over £5 to start my life in England.

It was many hours before we reached Paddington Station. I do not know where I got the idea that London was shiny and new. In the early morning mist, it was dark and dismal as we approached. The buildings on either side created a tunnel as we slowed our approach towards the station. The high buildings closed in on either side, back to back grey black buildings, covered in soot, from many years of pollution, created by the coal fires of the trains' steam engines. I asked a station guard, where to get the next train to Reading and he gave directions. I travelled for about one hour and came out of Reading Station, which was large and busy. I expected to be greeted by my sister but there was no-one there. I waited for about an hour. There were no mobile phones in those days so I sat in the sun with my suitcase and waited. No-one came.

As I reflect on those times I now see there was no communication between my sister and me. I was assuming she would know what time the train would arrive. This was not Limerick where everyone knew what time the boat train came in. A train from London to Reading came every hour. Mammy did all the letter writing to my sister. I have to say I did not read any of my sister's letters. I was not given them to read and if Mammy wanted me to know anything she would inform me. Mammy was heartbroken after Phillis left to do nursing. She cried for weeks. It was coming up towards Christmas when the song *I'm dreaming of a white Christmas* played on the radio. She would come in from the kitchen, sit down and cry into a clean tea towel. Christmas week we were all pretty miserable and the song came on the radio again. My younger brother said, "Wait!" He got a basin and said "have a good cry." We all started to laugh. Mammy dried her eyes and said, "It is not fair on everyone, me crying all the time at Christmas." I never saw her cry about Phillis again.

Chapter 7

Arrived

I realised no-one was coming for me, so I went back into the station to ask one of the staff, "Please can you tell me, how do I get to this address?" showing my sister's address that Mammy had given me. I had to take a trolleybus which was powered by electricity to the Wokingham Road. This was a new experience for me, as we did not have them in Limerick. There was a pole connecting the trolleybus to an electric wire. On the way to the trolleybus stop, I saw an African couple in their traditional dress. I was amazed, more at the lady's dress and headgear than their complexion, dark or fair skinned. My grandmother, who spent nine years in America, once told me that the nearer you came to the Equator the darker your skin was. It was a protection against the sun. The couple passed me I stopped and turned, as they went by my eyes following them. I had never seen people so colourfully dressed in Limerick, or met someone from the African sub-continent.

I had seen an Indian lady once in Woolworth's; a girl told me she was a princess. I could believe her, as the beautiful lady was dressed in a fine silk sari of exquisite colour.

I made my way to the address... It was a large house with a long garden; there were trees in shaded areas, with enormous branches, their green leaves throwing light and dark shadows on the lawn. The tree was such a welcome place to sit under on a hot summer's day. Children were playing and tables were being laid with homemade lemonade, little sandwiches and cakes. I later learned that the house was used as a nursery school run by two sisters. My sister rented a room on the third floor. The ladies told me my sister was out, so I asked if they needed help and busied myself, helping them lay the tables. It was a summer party for the students and parents.

Later my sister came with a friend. No apology was given for not meeting me at the station and she acted as if there was no problem. I quickly accepted that was how it was in England. She showed me her room and brought me next door to see Mrs Derberge. I had a room in her house. She was a very well educated, elderly lady. The rent was £3.10.00 per week, I handed it over leaving me little to carry on for the week. Mrs Derberge was in her seventies to eighties

Early on Monday morning I went into Reading, to a large supermarket and asked if they had any vacancies. The Human Resources lady took me to a room upstairs and asked me some maths questions, gave me some money, a till, groceries and asked me to ring up the items and give her the change There was an English girl there, who did not do so well on the change. The Human Resources lady offered me just over £5 per week and asked me when I would like to start work. I said now. She took me to the till in the supermarket and I started. She showed the other girl how to fill shelves. At break time I was shown the canteen, it was large and spacious. It was explained to me that you could have breakfast in the morning break, dinner at 1pm and tea and cake in the afternoon break. The canteen staff would make a note of what you had. The meals were subsidised.

When you got paid on Friday you would join a queue to get your pay packet as wages were paid in cash, you would then join another queue to pay for the food you got in the canteen. The food I ate in the canteen was sufficient food to last me the day. I bought a bottle of milk and biscuits to have for my supper, before I went to sleep. Sunday is a mystery to me. I don't remember much only that I did not cook and I certainly did not go to a restaurant. I found a Catholic church and went to Mass. I must have lunched on bread and cheese.

In the supermarket canteen I sat with Susan the girl who was interviewed with me and we became friendly. Susan invited me to her house. Her mother was kind and asked me if I would like to move in with her and the family. I said yes, as it was very quiet at Mrs Derberge's house. She went to bed early and it was so still and silent for the rest of the evening and night. I was not used to the silence.

I wrote a letter to Mammy; her reply was that Daddy had said, "Did Marie ever go to school?" My spellings were so bad. I have never been diagnosed with dyslexia, it is in my family. I always had a complex about my spellings that is why I would never consider being a secretary. If I try to sound out a word and spell it, it is nothing like it should be, when I attempt to write it down.

When I was about nine, at the end of the school year we would move up to the next class. This was a day we looked forward to. There was a hive of activity as one class would move up and then the next. I loved the first day in a new class. We were given books for the new school year. I loved the smell of new books, when you opened the pages for the first time. We would take them home and cover them with brown paper or wallpaper to keep the covers clean.

My class teacher was Sister Ann. She asked the class to stand up and said, "Follow me to the next class." She looked at me and said, "Not you Marie, sit down." I sat in the silence of the empty classroom for some time. The Reverend Mother passed the open door, she stopped and asked me,. "What are you doing there?" I said, "Sister Ann told me to wait in the classroom." She said, "Come with me" and took me to the next class. Sister Ann saw me and sent me back. The Reverend Mother was supervising in the corridor. She saw me come out of the class and she and Sister Ann had words. The outcome was the Reverend Mother lost and I stayed back in the same class for another year when I turned nine. I told Mammy what had happened and she went to the school to talk to the nuns. Sister Ann said I would gain by staying another year in her class. This is where Mammy would say, "Yes, Sister."

Little did Sister Ann know that I would not have to do any work to maintain my position in the class, which was in the middle where I would avoid the attention of the nuns. I knew I would be too old to stay back the next year. The trouble was I felt more mature then the other children in the class. There was dyslexia in our family although not all were affected. It is a brain condition that causes difficulty in reading and spelling. Little was known about it at the time, I believe the nuns knew nothing about it as it was never mentioned. I was never tested for it. I would have to learn to spell a word as I could not make a guess at it. I seemed to hear it differently; small words seemed to be more of a problem than big ones. I was shy and very embarrassed if the nun asked me to read in class. It was a time when children were seen and not heard. She would start the children reading with the first girl in the row; by the time she got to me, I was in a panic. I would get red in the face, until she asked me to sit down. I could read to myself very well. Maths was not a problem. I would work out the sum and come to the correct answer. However, if a nun pointed to me in mental arithmetic I would panic and my brain would shut down.

It rarely happened, but one day we had a substitute teacher. The Reverend Mother took our class. We were told to take out our books and Sister questioned the class on the work set by the class teacher the previous day. Some children looked blank and she decided to ask Mary Rose, a good student who always did her homework. Mary Rose could not answer. The Reverend Mother said she was very disappointed in her. Mary Rose burst into tears; I was horrified as I did not do much homework, if any. I relied on what I remembered in class to get me through the day. That is if I was not daydreaming or in a trance. Not that I did not worry when I lay in bed on a Sunday night and I did not do my English or Irish essays. I sometimes wished that I did not wake up in the morning but that I died in the night... That incident reinforced my opinion about sticking my head out and being noticed. Sailing along as I was doing, suited me

My friend Susan from work was a twin, I do not think the twins were identical as they were very different in personality. Susan's sister's name was Ann. She seemed quieter and a little more intelligent. Her mother and father were divorced. One day the twins had a row and my friend ripped up a collection of greeting postcards her sister Ann had. I could not believe that she could do such a cruel thing, as Ann was proud of her collection and had them pinned to her bedroom wall. Her mother did not get involved in the argument which I found strange as I thought some punishment was in order...

When there was a programme on animal cruelty on the television the mother would rant and rave. She became quiet scary, but when she saw the shock look on my face she justified her rant by saying, she loved animals. At the time there was a movement towards awareness and flower power. This was a passive resistance in the Sixties and Seventies to animal cruelty and other issues.

The mother had a man friend who stopped outside their house in a grey van. I did not know what he looked like, as he never came into the house and I never got a glimpse of him. She would join him for a chat. One night we were looking out the window and one of the sisters asked if the van was 'rocking and rolling' again. They laughed. I did not offer comment as I did not know what they were talking about. They were a strange family in my view.

One weekend my friend's mother asked me to accompany her to a mental hospital; her son was a patient there. I had not heard mention of him before. When we got to the shop near the hospital, which was a tobacconist's, she said, "Buy something for him, it will cheer him up." I bought him a pipe and tobacco. His mother thought that was a good idea. All the way to the hospital she was saying, "His father put him in the mental hospital, it is all his father's fault. That is why he is there"

The hospital was a very grey, dismal place. We entered a long ward with older men sitting in chairs beside their beds or in their beds propped up with their pillows. He was in a bed towards the end of the ward. It was visiting time and there were a few visitors. I was surprised that he was only a little older than me. The other men started calling out to him. "Is that your girlfriend, Joe?" He was very withdrawn and shy.

Chapter 8

Shepherd's Bush

One weekend, I visited my sister. I saw my older sister as a surrogate mother; she was tall, slim and blonde. Phillis spoke with an English accent. She was the opposite of me. She had a knack of lighting up a room when she entered. She was bright and intelligent. She came to England when she was sixteen. A cousin of my Mammy's was the Reverend Mother of a convent and the matron of a hospital in Cardiff. Phillis started as a cadet nurse and went on to study nursing. A matter of weeks after I arrived in England, Phillis said to me, "I am moving to London." She had to leave nursing, as she contracted tubercular glands in her stomach. After treatment to cure the disease, her health was declared sound once more. Phillis stayed for a short time in Reading. She was advised by the doctor and medical staff to leave nursing. The work would damage her health and she could no longer handle the changing shift, from nights to days and the long hours. The doctor told her if she left nursing for some years, she could return to her studies when she was stronger. That is if she wished.

I arrived as an uninvited guest. She had her plans which had not included me. It must never have been her intention to remain in Wokingham; she no longer did nursing and had to find alternative work. She had plans to move to London where the chance of a good office job was better. She did not feel the necessity to discuss it in detail with me as she had been living away from home since she was sixteen; it had made her very independent.

It must have been very hard for her when she was ill, as I later saw the medication she had to take; she was twenty-four with two children when she had a relapse. The tablets were large, white and hard to swallow. When Phillis was sick Mammy wrote to a good friend of hers, who lived in the UK and she and her husband went to visit Phillis. It was not the same as having a visit from a member of one's family. I felt at the time a little deserted by her leaving me but I was excited with the prospect of joining her in London. She was right to go to London for work. The chances of getting a good office job were greater in London than Reading.

She rented a room in Shepherd's Bush. On my first visit, we went to her friend's sister, Monica, who had a flat on the Goldhawk Road. Her friend Bernie was from Trinidad and had been nursing with Phillis. Monica was a teacher, who lived with her husband and daughter. There were a lot of nurses coming and going as they seemed to use the flat as a London base, while working in hospitals around England. Her husband was not a happy man; he was complaining about the telephone bill and putting a lock on the phone. The nurses had run up a large phone bill.

The food was very foreign to me; I ate breakfast cereal and chocolate for the Sunday. I returned on Monday morning to Reading on the fast train in time for work.

My sister said she would come with a car for me on the following Saturday to collect her things and take me to London. She had left an assortment of books, crockery and utensils with me until she settled. I was very pleased to join her and had my brown case packed and ready from early Saturday morning. I waited and waited. Around 10pm that night, Susan's mother said that her husband had threatened to withhold her maintenance, as I was staying at the house and was giving her money. I would have to go. I left my sister's boxes. I told Susan's mother that my sister would come for the boxes; I bade the family a quiet farewell.

I walked along the dark street of the estate. This was the first time that the silent tears flowed, as I made my way along the road to the bus stop and station. I was lucky to get the last Reading to London train. I do not know what I was crying about, disappointment over not being picked up or a sense of isolation and loneliness. Maybe both. I was not going home, that would be defeatist...

I arrived at Paddington and took the underground train to Shepherd's Bush to where my sister's room was. The West

Indian landlord opened the door. He must have thought it was strange to see someone so young call so late. It was a very hot summer's night and after midnight. I did not think of that at the time. He looked at me and said, "Your sister is out but if you wanted to leave your suitcase you can." I told him, "I will go to my sister's friend, tell my sister I will see her in the morning." I walked to Goldhawk Road which was not far and knocked long and loud on the door.

The flat was on the second floor, above a shop. After some time a window opened and a very dark, very large West Indian lady put her head out and called, "Yes, what you want?" I told her I was Phillis's sister. She came down and let me in. It was the night of the Trinidad Independence Dance which would have been around 31st August, 1962. The flat was deserted but for her, as they were all at the celebration dance. She said, "Your sister no longer lives in that house and the landlord had no right to take your case." I told her, "I will collect it in the morning." She said, "Phillis will be here in the morning. You will see her then. You are welcome to stay the night if you do not mind sharing." Olive was the nurse's name. She did not go to the dance as she was on early shift in the morning. I slept with Olive that night. She was very kind to me and gave me advice about saving my money and not spending it like my sister. I did not tell her that my small wages did not allow me to save. There was little enough to survive on. Phillis came with a friend on Sunday morning. I told her what had happened and that I would go for my case.

I knocked on the door of Phillis's previous landlord. He would not give me my suitcase; he said he was keeping it for compensation as my sister had left a dirty sheet in her room. His wife came out as I tried to protest that it was my case and not my sister's. The wife started making noises in the background so I left and went back to the flat. I was trembling, I had a pink cotton dress on and it was wet with perspiration. Monica's husband said he would ring the police for me. He said, "You can explain what happened and arrange to meet them at the top of the landlord's road, because if the police saw me, they may not do anything for you."

I went to the top of the road and the police car arrived and we walked to the house.

Now the wife started to scream and go crazy, you would think I'd brought people to murder her. She shouted at the top of her voice, "Look, she brought police for us." The policeman said to her husband, "Tell your wife to go inside the house." He looked at her and shouted, "Go inside, woman!" She went inside... By this time we had an audience on the street: One or two men sitting on the low walls outside their houses; women, their front doors opened wide, standing on the steps, which led from the door to the road. Their arms were folded as they enjoyed the commotion. The officer turned to the neighbours. He said loudly "Go back inside your homes. There is nothing happening here that is any of your business." The crowd dispersed.

He asked me, "Do you have any identification inside the suitcase?"I had been to a church youth club in Reading, I told the officer. "I had a membership card in a small purse, my name is on it." The officer checked, he said to the landlord, "You have no quarrel with this lady, you have to give her back her suitcase." As the officer and I walked back up the road towards the officer's car he said to me, "Keep away from these people, you can see how they are." I was just glad to get my suitcase with all my worldly possessions back. I thanked him and we went our separate ways.

Chapter 9

Visit To The Nurses' Home

My sister's friend invited me to pay a visit to the hospital, where she and my sister did their nursing. I made my way by bus. Bernie was there to meet me. She introduced me to the matron, who asked me if I was going to study nursing like my sister. I said no.

I had played with the idea of being a nurse when I was little, as all young girls do. I remember looking longingly in the window of a toy shop, on a crisp winter's days, leading up to Christmas. I was well dressed in my hat and gloves and warm coat. There was a children's nurse's uniform in blue with a red cross on the front, a red cape and a white nurse's cap. There was also a nurse's bag, opened to show a thermometer and injection needle. I never asked my Mammy for it. If I asked for it I thought she would say, "Where would I get the money from?" Maybe I would have got it, if I'd asked.

I had just escaped from school and I was not going back to the classroom again. I was shown around the hospital and the nurses' quarters. I was introduced to nurses we met along the way, as Phillis's sister. The nurses' rooms were small and cell-like. They were brightened up with personal items and made to feel as homely as was possible.

We made our way to the canteen. I looked at a blackboard on the wall where the menu was written in white chalk. I saw Welsh Rabbit also known as Welsh Rarebit and thought I might try that. I sat down at a table with my tray and examined my plate. I could see no meat. I asked my sister's friend Bernie where was the meat. She laughed and told me it was toast with a cheese sauce I was disappointed as I needed something more substantial. I did not want to seem greedy by going up for another meal. I had never heard the name Welsh Rabbit, in our house.

After getting my suitcase back, my sister and I made our way to Westbourne Grove in Ladbroke Grove where she had rented a room. I unpacked my small case and moved in. Phillis was always dressed smartly. She had a lovely expensive cotton blouse that she would wash when she came from work, it would be dried by the gas fire and ironed so it was new and fresh in the morning. Her bad habit was she smoked. When she woke in the morning, she put her glasses on and groped behind the bed head ledge for her cigarettes.

I did not smoke. I will tell you how I managed to make the decision not to smoke. At school my friends and I met up in the playground during break and arranged to walk home together. There was a buzz in the air as one of my friends had a secret and would not tell us until our walk home from school. Heads close together, we walked up the hill, a group of young schoolgirls chatting. My friend had a packet of five cigarettes in her school bag; we were going to try smoking them. I suggested we go to Farranshone. There was an old tennis court and a passage leading to it, situated at the back of the Ennis Road, behind the houses, where we would not be seen by neighbour. They would tell us off and tell our mothers. We settled in a corner, bags, coats and school hats, thrown on the ground, all eyes on my friend as she opened the box of cigarettes with great ceremony. She passed one to each of us in turn. A match was struck and we lit up, puffing away, a cloud of smoke escaping from every mouth. We were trying to make as much smoke as possible, opening and closing our mouths like a steam engine trying to make little puffs. We finished our cigarettes and parted, as it was known by parents how long it took you to get home from school. We did not want Mammies to get suspicious and ask, what took you so long. We had done the deed; there was no need to comment on it, or say we must try again.

When I arrived home Daddy was reading the paper sitting in his chair by the fire. I came and said hello. He often said in Irish how was school every day. I corrected his grammar saying, how was school today, as I often did. He never got it right. He must have noticed the smell of the cigarette, as he asked me to take Mammy's cigarettes from behind the clock on the mantelpiece, where she kept them. She always maintained that she smoked

five a day. That was not true it was more like ten. She said they
calmed her nerves. Daddy then took out his handkerchief and
said, "Marie, let me show you this." He lit the cigarette and took
a puff and blew the smoke through the handkerchief. It left a
brown mark, he then said, "You can imagine what your Uncle
Bob's lungs are like, he is a chain smoker." I did not say much as
Daddy said, "Is that the time? I must go back to work." The very
thought of having my lungs brown and smelly with smoke was
enough to put me off for life. That night my appetite for my
supper was diminished. I liked my food so cigarettes were not for
me.

In the mornings it was a mad rush for Phillis to get out the
door for work. The next day I walked up Portobello Road and
found Woolworth's. I applied for a job and had no problem
getting it. That weekend my sister and I went to Monica's. She
was having a party still celebrating Trinidad Independence. A
young man spoke to me. He was in his early twenties. He knew
my sister. He asked me how I was settling in to London life and
had I got a job yet. I was never one to hold back when asked a
direct question. I said I'd got a job at Woolworth's in Portobello
Road and I started Monday.

At Woolworth's the supervisor took me to the counter
where I would work. It was near the entrance doors to
Portobello Road. He showed me the ice cream section and
proceeded to show me how to operate the ice cream machine.
Then, who should appear in my peripheral vision with another
young man, my friendly young man from the party. The
supervisor finished showing me what to do and went away. The
young man I met at the party introduced John to me. He said
that he was a friend of my sister and could I give him the number
of the house where she lived, as he had lost touch. I thought she
will kill me. She was quiet capable of doing it. I gave them the
wrong house number. I hoped that would be the end of that.

From about three pm I saw him walking up and down
outside the shop. I came out at six pm. He met me and said he
would walk down with me to the house. I was shaking in my
shoes. When my sister met him she made such a fuss of him,
treated him like he was a long, lost brother. He presented her
with chocolate and fruit. I breathed a sigh of relief as I thought

he had a passion for her. I was glad the heat was off me. John came a few times more; always bringing gifts to my sister. I was not greatly impressed by him. He never had a lot to say to me when he came. He visited Woolworth's on Saturday dressed in his dark blue cashmere suit. He looked so handsome. I was hooked and then he asked me to the cinema. There was also another boy that asked me to the cinema. I asked my sister who I should go out with, she was in favour of John. He was a Trinidadian young man of Indian descent.

How can I say what attracts me to John? Was it a chemical reaction? I just do not know. I have looked the word 'love' up in the dictionary: "Love is a force of nature, you cannot demand love or take it away." I knew I belonged with John. I can best describe John as about five foot eight inches tall and handsome. He had a strong Trinidadian accent, which he never lost. He was presentable and well dressed. I admired the fact he was hardworking and careful with money. I felt secure with him. I could not consider a man that could fritter away his money and not pay his way in life. He never used bad language, inside or out of the house. There was confidence in his bearing. My thinking was a boy who was good to his mother would be good to his wife and children. He was streetwise at a time when it was very necessary. Sharp as a razor, very bright and intelligent, he could pick things up very easily. He lacked a formal education as he would leave school in the fruit-picking season, to pick oranges on an estate and box them. When he got paid he would buy two pairs of shorts and shirts for school, a toy and sweets for his younger siblings, then return to school. He was strong both in character and physical strength. His upbringing did not allow for shows of wild affection. Children in his family had to help with the work on the land and in the house. He held strong Victorian values and was strict in his dealings with family, coming from a large family as he did, where it was not regarded as manly to show weakness or the softer side of his nature. No task was hard for him. He would rise early in the morning and attend to whatever task he had planned to do that day. I knew he loved me by his actions. When he left early for work he would put the pillow at my back so I would continue sleeping for a little while before the start of my day, getting the children ready for school and me off to work.

I made friends with a girl I met when I first started work in Woolworth's. One day an Irish lady came to my counter. She said she had a house nearby with a room to let. The rent was high so I asked her if my friend could share. I told her my friend worked on another counter. I directed her to where she worked. I told her that she was from Trinidad. She asked me if she was dark. I said no she was Indian.

I tended to be in the way very much with my sister, she had a friend and was used to her own space. I told her about the room. she seemed quite happy to let me go. Judy was my friends name and she was also looking for a room, she was of mixed parentage, an Indian mother and Chinese father. She was a very pretty girl. The Irish lady went to have a look at her and said we could have the room.

Chapter 10

New Year's Eve 1962

Winter in London Town

John had made friends with two boys, Ian and Robert. Robert was from Somerset and Ian was a Londoner. They were on leave at the time from the Royal Engineers. We would go out together as a group. I was sharing a room with Judy at the time. It was around New Year's Eve 1962, snow started to fall from Boxing Day and there was a big freeze until March, 1963. The winter freeze came again in the winter of 1963. The Thames froze at Windsor. The lake in St James Park was also frozen.

I never remember it being so cold in Limerick. When it was a frosty, icy night it was a time of joy. I remember sitting in the fireside chair dreaming of many wonderful things, mesmerised by the ambers from a turf and coal fire, oranges, reds and blues dancing on the coals, glowing to perfection bringing me warmth and comfort after a troublesome day at school.

My peace was shattered by my brother Chris who rushed in with the news that Farranshone had ice on the road and we would be skating. Chris and I had many adventures together.

I was out of that chair in a second and made my way up the road.

The stars spread a tapestry of silver patterns on the darkened frosty night, the hedges and trees had a frosty appearance, the twinkling stars had one or two falling stars. My mother said that when you saw a shooting star it meant a soul went to heaven. I thought not many go to heaven then; it was not appropriate to tell her. The full moon reflected off the black ice, it became our street lamp and lit up the road.

A bucket of water and a sweeping brush insured a proper icy run. Children formed a line outside No 6 Farranshone. The icy run started there and finished at our house, No 12. Shoes were inspected by the big boys, the soles of our shoes had to be leather as rubber would melt the ice

I failed the inspection as the soles of my shoes were rubber and I doubted that I could acquire a pair of leather shoes. I headed home to search through a pile of old shoes. There were no shoes that fitted me; at last I found a pair much bigger than my size. I once again made my way clip-clopping up the road to join the queue of hopeful children.

I passed inspection and was then allowed to go on the ice. I took off at a run clip-clopping down the road lifting my heavy shoes; put my best foot forward crouching a little down the icy path, hands outstretched to keep my balance. I went slivering and sliding past houses and came off the ice at a run outside my house. Repeating the action once again clip-clopping back up the road and joining the queue for my next run. Cold did not exist for us with glowing cheeks and happy hearts.

There were not many cars on our road in those days and our fun came to an abrupt end when a driver tried to control his car on the black ice. There was much shouting out of the window of his car about reporting us to the Guards, after that, the moment was gone and we made our way back to our homes and bed.

The sport was superb. I dreamed of moving at a record breaking speed down the icy road; another winter's evening passed successfully in Farranshone.

John's friend Ian was a kind boy. He had to return to his base and wanted his grandmother to have company on New Year's Eve. He invited Judy and I to visit her in London. She was very kind to us; she had prepared a high tea, laid out on the table, a beautiful tea service in fine-boned china. There were little sandwiches of ham and tomato and egg in salad cream. There was a tin of biscuits with a Christmas scene and holly on the lid. Also, a Christmas cake iced and sprinkled with silver balls, a snowman and children on a sledge on the top. She entertained us with stories of London during the war until it got quite late, as we bid her farewell, we noticed the weather conditions had worsened. We took the train back home. The snowfall was getting heavier. It was the 31st December 1962. Our train stopped at Kensington and could go no further. Judy and I came out of the station to see silent snow softly falling in great quantities of crystalline flakes. Snowflakes always fascinate me. They start as a tiny cloud droplet freezing into a hexagonal prism. Snowflakes covered every surface within our vision. All was silent except for the crunch under our feet. We should have been scared as we had no means of transport and not any idea of how to get home. Youth is ever optimistic. We made our way in high excitement.

I do not remember Limerick ever having such heavy snow. I remembered coming back home from midnight Mass with Mammy, wishing that it would snow and we would have a fairy tale Christmas, enough snow for Santa to come on his sledge.

Judy, coming from Trinidad, was experiencing it for the first time. I put my hand out and let the snow fall on it, in white crystallised flakes with their mystical patterns, a myriad of shapes. The shapes of snowflakes are determined by the temperature and humidity, when they are formed.

We trudged along occasionally passing couples and small groups on their way home, some throwing snowballs at one another. They had abandoned public transport like us. They would wave to us and call out "Happy New Year!" We would wave back and sometimes we would call out, "Are we heading in the right direction for Notting Hill Gate?" They would give us directions and so we made our way home enjoying every moment of our magical journey.

I moved in to Camilford Road with John. The living conditions there were bad. Our house had a bathroom which consisted of an iron bath sitting on two planks of wood, in a derelict cellar. One night while having a bath, I thought I heard someone moving in the basement area. I called out, but silence reigned. I felt somebody was watching. They could stand outside the window in the area and look in. There were no curtains on the window. The lights always seemed so dim. I speeded up and made haste to leave the bath and escape to my room.

That incident scared me and put me off using the bath in our house. I asked John to ask a neighbour he knew who had a house in the neighbourhood, if we could use his bath. He agreed.

Johanne was a French girl who lived in our house. One night Johanne and I set out to the neighbours, to have our bath. It was a foggy night. As soon as we put our foot across the threshold, we realised the fog was bad. We could not see the lower part of our body, or our hands, stretched out in front of us. The direction to the house was, to the bottom of the road then left until we reached the end of that road, not a long distance. In good visibility, five minutes at most.

The silence was eerie. All traffic was at a standstill, not even a man on a bicycle was abroad. Our voices hung in the air. We called out. "Is there anybody there?"

No answers. It called to mind how it was in the time of Jack the Ripper's 1888 just 74 years before. We talked about him in low hushed voices, not wanting to give a ghostly listener any ideas.

Time stood still for us, our walk slow and stilted. We were now suddenly cast into blindness without training or warning. We could not see the end of our road or where to turn left. With the open road the smog was more dense. We were in the middle of a blanket of smog that entirely covered London and the country. Making our way slowly, we held on to the railings of the Victorian houses.

We were so relieved to get to our destination. We knocked on the door and announced to a tenant of the house, we had come for a bath. She just pointed in the direction of the bathroom without comment.

There was no point in Johanne or I waiting on one another to have our separate baths, at a cost of two shillings to the gas meter, we put one shilling in, opened the taps, watched while the water gushed from the silver taps. We slipped out of our clothes and quickly immersed ourselves in the clear bath water. It was a large, long, iron bath. We lingered in the warmth, topping up with hot water as it cooled, chatting away like sisters, unconcerned about our nakedness. I was trying to figure out why all lights gave a dim soft light at the time, in all rented houses. The landlord would have put the lowest wattage to save on the electricity bill.

With a blast of light from the gas, when we topped up the hot water and the steady glow from the pilot light, reflecting the ripples of bath water, it gave a soft yellow light, which was cosy and comforting. Our thoughts were to linger as long as we could before we faced the arduous journey home. This was the London smog of early December 1962. Seven hundred and fifty more deaths than usual were reported. London hospital emergency services were on alert.

Chapter 11

I Sent A Photograph Home

I wanted to make our relationship official, so John and I went to a photographer to make sure it was recorded by an official photograph. We dressed to impress. None of my photos taken with a small camera would do. I took my time to write to Mammy. I wrote to say John and I were getting engaged. I do not know if that constitutes permission to wed. I can be forthright when I am trying to get a message over. They did not know at the time that I had moved in with John.

London was a scary place on your own. I was ready to nest, make a home for the two of us. My instinct, without fully understanding it was to look for the strongest male, who could love and protect me.

We as humans are no different than animals. They look for a good gene pool. They choose the healthiest and the strongest to carry on their generation.

I would not have liked to be a fly on the wall when my letter arrived. I can only imagine what my father's reaction was, when he saw the photograph. It was all down to John's complexion which was dark and my age.

Little did I know that John's mother would feel the same. She had sent John to England to work, to send money home to improve their lives. He had to return the money she had invested in him. She did not send him to take on the responsibility of a wife and family. They had a saying in Trinidad, 'She will back a truck, take everything and go'. There was the feeling that he would lose every little gain he made.

Mammy was on the next boat over. She arrived and there had to be a reshuffle of our living arrangements. My sister seemed not to be in trouble. I had to be the one who sent the photograph. My Mammy said I must come home for a holiday. She was not going back without me, she did not say so but I knew. We left from Paddington and my sister's friend was there to wave us goodbye. He told Mammy not to let me come back. After a long train ride, we boarded the boat. It was a stormy night. I noticed the crew putting brown paper bags on all the tables. I hadn't noticed that before. I said to Mammy, "It looks like it will be a bad passage." She told me, she had been to see a very interesting film and she would tell me all about it. It would take our minds off the movement of the boat which left the harbour. Mammy stopped mid-sentence with her story and made a hasty retreat towards the bathroom. She did not make it and was sick outside one of the crew's cabins. She came back very embarrassed and looking poorly. A little girl, who was running around at first, now sat in silence, looking very grey, on her parents' suitcase. I looked around; it looked like a hospital ship. I felt good until we reached calm waters on the Irish side. Then I felt sick. It was cold and damp when we disembarked.

When I arrived home I settled in and kept my head down. Daddy said I was not going back. I worked on Mammy. I could be logical in my arguments and she eventually let me go back to England when Daddy was at work. I headed back to England and John. Daddy gave Mammy a very hard time, after I left.

I went to work at Wall's Bacon factory at that time. On the first afternoon of work, near finishing time I was called to the personnel office and asked if I wanted a sub. I said no, I was fine. It was their custom to give a sub of the first day's pay to emigrants so that they could have money to pay travel to work and feed themselves until they got paid on Friday. It seems strange calling the Irish emigrants but that is what we were. We were referred to as the Irish or Paddies.

The supervisor put me on a training line. I had to sit high over a moving production line with a weighing scale designed with a thin hand. I would have to place the bacon slices on the hand. To measure the weight exactly, you slip a Wall's bag over the hand, turn it over, slip it off and drop it down on the moving line. The problem was it never weighed the eight ozs. You had to cut a small piece and hide it behind a slice of bacon. I wanted the weight to be perfect. That took time. If you did a thousand a day, you would get a bonus for over and above. The most I did was four hundred. I soon realised I was not suited for this kind of work. I could not go automatic.

Some time passed, I started to feel unwell on the way to work, when the bus went up over and down the hill. I realised I was safer walking the last stretch. I went to the medical department. The nurse asked, "Could you be pregnant?" I said "Yes."

Chapter 12

Cousin Peter

My cousin Peter arrived from Ireland. My sister Phillis looked after him at first. He settled in very quickly, got a job as a salesman in a men's store in Queensway and got a room. I was just a few months older than him. We were brought up like sister and brother. Our mothers were twins and they were never far apart. People assumed we were twins. They would ask how old are you? I would say I was four months older than Peter. They would look in amazement. I would say we were cousins and everyone relaxed.

His Mammy, my aunt paid a visit. We went to dinner with her in a restaurant in Queensway. During the dessert I could taste that the cream was off, as my sense of taste was heightened due to my pregnancy, so I went to the restroom. My sister Phillis followed me. She said to me, "I have something to tell you. I am pregnant. "I said to her, "So am I." We looked at one another in stunned silence. I was not expecting that. We returned to our aunt. She had come over to bring her son home. She told him his father was ill to encourage him to go home with her. I am sure Peter was upset when he got home as he would not have the money to come back. He met a girl, got a job, got married and settled down to life at home. My aunt loved her son. He was her pride and joy. He was an only child for about nine or ten years before his brother came along.

I remember him to be very spoilt as a child.

Which brings me back to his behaviour on the day of my first communion. Leading up to our big day the nuns had us working very hard on our Catechism with threats that if we did not know the answer we would fail and not make our first Holy Communion. There was practice at the church with wafers and our first confession. My sins were not helping my Mammy and fighting with my siblings. They were the same sins repeated for many a year after. It seemed to work. There were rumours that if your sins were bad you would have to say the rosary and every one would know, because they would go back to school and you would still be kneeling in church finishing the rosary. I was lucky I got three Hail Marys.

The week of the First Communion was a very expensive time. It was very busy with visits to town. I had to get new socks, panties, vest, bodice, slip, white dress, veil and white shoes, white sateen bag, a bouquet of flowers, prayer book and rosary beads. We went to all the shops and purchased what was needed. On Saturday afternoon the last thing was my shoes... As most of the schools in Limerick made their First Communion on the same day there were no white shoes that fitted me properly. I settled for a pair that squeezed my toes afraid to say they did not fit in case I could not make my communion

On the day I was dressed in my First Communion regalia, I felt like a princess. I thought that mine was the nicest dress and veil of all. I did not need to look at anyone else. I was walking on air. We were not allowed to eat from the night before. It was common for some children to feel faint, I was told to put my head between my knees if I felt faint. I thought that was a bit extreme but I tried it out anyway. The Mass seemed long and I remember having a little chat with my neighbour about my sateen purse and doing a comparison.

The children were in rows, girls at one side and boys at the other. There would be no contamination with the nuns. Thirty or more of us all together. After our First Communion the boys went to a boys' school and our school was a girls' school from that year on. It felt like we were going through a rite of passage and now we had arrived. Floating up to the altar in our shimmering white dresses and veils with boys in new suits with their white rosette badge. We looked like a host of angels on the celestial globe.

When we came out of the church we had photographs taken. I was given some silver coins to put in my silk purse. Next were the visits to close relatives with ice cream and lemonade for me, tea and cake for my parents. Each visit I had an addition to my purse. My aunty and Cousin Peter came with us on our visits and I took note that Peter had been given the same coin as me, even though he did not make his communion. More pictures were taken in the People's park in Pery Square where Peter got fed up with the whole scene and had a tantrum. My feet were squeezing me by this time. I could have given him a thump, he was an only child and we had a house full of children. I was used to putting up and shutting up.

From there Daddy decided he needed refreshments, so we went to a hotel bar. I got a glass of orange juice frosted around the top with a slice of orange pierced to the lip of the glass. It was so grown up. Looking around me and taking in the scene, I saw a man, the sunlight hitting off his glass, the colour was so rich and deep. I could not take my eyes off its jewel like ruby red colours inter-changing between light and dark. I thought it must be cherry in flavour. I asked my Daddy for a glass, I really wanted one. He said no. I offered to pay for it. Daddy said it was only for grown-ups.

The next day my silk purse was lying on the table empty, my Mammy would have put the money towards the cost of my first communion clothes. I accepted the loss without question as in my view, I had gained so much.

My aunt and cousin came to visit all my Daddy's family with my mother and father. This was our custom. My Daddy's sisters would have said bring Marie up to see us on her First Communion day. I would be given some silver for my little white sateen purse.

Chapter 13

Mammy Arrived Over Again

Mammy arrived over again, probably prompted by the success of Peter's return. She said I looked pale and come home for a rest. I was cornered. I had to go. I went to the doctor for tablets, so I would not be sick. That was a dangerous time as pregnant women were prescribed Thalidomide tablets to relieve their symptoms which caused deformity in thousands of births.

When I was alone at home I secured my birth certificate, then I went to the island to see my Granny. I asked her to look after my money and certificate. John had given me money to pay my passage to come back. If my Mammy found it she would have taken it, so that I could not return to the UK. Granny said nothing but went upstairs with it. There was a big row when my father came home one day. I had never seen him so angry. He said some unkind words and if he saw me near the train station he would push me under the train... The Magdalena Sisters were still active at that time. I remember being told if I did not behave I would be sent there. They would put some manners on me. I knew they had a laundry. I did not know until it was made public, what happened to girls who got into trouble.

I am anxious here to let you know the status of my father's mind on receiving the photograph of John and me. I was requesting permission for us to get engaged and married. I sent a photograph of both of us. You could not get married without your parents' consent until you were twenty-one.

My father was a well-read man. He read about the movement for integration with the African-American. He would have known how they suffered under slavery and would have read *To kill a mocking bird* It was their long hard struggle towards emancipation. The Sixties was a time when it was well publicised: Their struggle for equal rights. He would have heard about

Martin Luther King Jr. His Civil Rights movement and later on 27th August 1963 his speech (*I have a dream where each person would be judged on their character and not on the colour of their skin*).

He would have known of the British Raj, the status of the British Raj with their Memsahibs in India and their British rule over the population of India.

He was one of a generation who were not openly prejudiced, as it was not necessary. There were very few foreigners in our town. It was more of a class consciousness in Ireland at that time. He could not consider his daughter marrying an outsider. He did not want a daughter to suffer a life of struggle by association. He wanted his daughter to marry a man who was a good provider, an educated man and finally an Irishman. Then he could relax, his duty done. He could bask under the tree of the seed he had planted so many years ago.

Let me give you a romantic view about Daddy. After supper on a Saturday night when Daddy came home, he would sometimes be in a mellow mood. He would have paid a visit to his local pub. While there, he would have partaken of refreshments offered by the establishment, Guinness with a whiskey chaser. It was important not to rush the Guinness. The barman would let it rest on the bar until the head stood proud on top of the rich black Guinness, like an Irish coffee. The whiskey chaser could be drunk while admiring the settling of the Guinness that is if funds permitted. When Daddy got older he had a seat in a pub called Lanny Frazer's he enjoyed sitting in it. If it was occupied and the person sitting there did not know it was his seat the bar man would see Daddy entering the Pub and say to the unfortunate Man, "get up and give Mr G.... his seat" and the chair would be vacated. Younger men had to respect the older heads as they were referred to, or they would not be welcomed by the publican.

When Daddy came home he also had his chair by the fire, which was vacated by his children, when he entered the house. He would sit by the fire on a Saturday night and put his hand on his heart saying, "I am not long for this world." He had a problem with his heart, however he lived to a grand old age. He would continue with *"Bury me in Ross Na-Ri and face me towards the rising sun."* A poem for the Burial of Ard Ri (King Cormac the

First AD266 poem by Dr Ferguson)... Daddy loved poetry and could quote from many great authors and poets. The trouble was he never said they were quotes. I was under the impression that they were his sayings.

He would relate stories about his childhood and his father's farm called Capahard in Ennis, County Clare, where he would go as a young boy and spend summer holidays. He would tell us stories about his youth; his Uncle Paddy who was a horse whisperer. Daddy would say he was very good with horses. His aunts were churchgoing and religious women.

One day a cow was drowned in the bog land on the farm, despite all their efforts to save it. It was such a loss both in the effort to save the cow and the financial loss to the family.

He would tell us ghost stories that were passed down in his family. Then he would move on to tell stories about when he sang opera in Venice. He said, "When I pass under the balcony of the beautiful ladies in my gondola, they would throw roses to me." He would chuckle at the thought of the scene going through his mind. We also heard from him about walking the Great Wall of China and many other adventures. Years later my brother was in China on business and walked the Great Wall and got a certificate in my father's name. Daddy enjoyed this very much.

We would sit around the fire and absorb every word that Daddy said. They became stories that we loved; it was hard to separate fact from fiction. Mammy would come in from the kitchen drying her hands on a tea towel saying, "He was never out of this country." She would say it in a good-natured way. We all smiled as we knew that she had been listening to the stories in the kitchen while she was working. She waited until the story was finished before she made a comment. We all knew they were stories but were not sure if the stories were true or not.

Years later when I read more extensively I came across a lot of his sayings and was amazed to see where they came from. I smiled to think he was infiltrating the book I was reading, bringing back memories of the first time I heard the quote, *"The feeling of wellbeing that surrounded me, of capturing a moment in my youth."* One of his favourite quotes, when referring to the gathering at Lanny Fraser's pub. *"And still they gazed and still the wonder grew, that one small head could carry all he knew."* It was *The Village Schoolmaster* by Oliver Goldsmith. He would tap his head to indicate his store of knowledge followed by a chuckle. He thought that was very funny. Another of his was, *"To thine own self be true and it must follow as the night the day thou cannot be false to any man"* by Polonius in *Hamlet.* He once said to me as we were going to church, I was thinking of leaving school at the time. "The technical school has very good courses on offer; you should go and talk to them." I thought, *why do you not go yourself if you are so keen on it, I am happy the way I am. I did not dare to say that to him.*

Chapter 14

Choir Night

I joined the choir in the Franciscans Church to be able to go into town on practice nights. It was the only way I could stay out late, or go into town at night. Choir practice was on Thursday night and afterwards I would meet up with my friends. I have to admit I enjoyed singing and sang at two Masses on Sunday at 11.15am and 12pm. I loved church music in Latin and though I never learned the language properly, I could manage the songs in Latin, singing in the choir. I had a few favourites, *Panis Angelicus* and the *Ave Maria*. When we'd finished I would meet my friends in the Cafe Capri for expresso coffee. They would be sitting in a booth of red leather, boys and girls. I would order my cup of coffee, making sure I left a little in the bottom, for when the waitress came round and was about to throw us out. We would say we had not finished. We would laugh, gossip, ignore the call from the boys, talk about a very handsome, out of reach, older boy. That coffee had to last us for a very long time, as we did not have any more money.

When we had no money, which was often, we would hang out at my friend Sorcha's house or Hanna's house. Sorcha's mother was a lovely lady; she got the message eventually that we had no money and gave Sorcha money so she had enough to pay sixpence each, for a trip to the cafe and a cup of coffee. I always thought it was so kind of her, as she was on her own with her daughter. I thought my parents could afford to give me money. I had stopped asking or maybe I did not ask as I knew the struggles Mammy had with money. Now I realise that Mammy had seven children to feed, clothe and put through school.

Off we would go to the cafe, stopping for Hanna along the way. Hanna lived over their music shop. We would go in her room and chat, tell jokes which made her laugh so heartily that she would run to the toilet. She had kidney stones but not diagnosed at the time. We would find more jokes to make her laugh that would send us into hysterics.

Then we would go to the cafe, into a red leather booth, order our coffee. We would be greeted by people we knew; one or two passing our booth would linger for a chat. Boys would call to us; we would ignore them, as if they were a nuisance. We were pleased they noticed us. We were happy to be in one another's company. During Lent we had to go to church, to do a week of sermons, some of the missionary priests preached hell fire and damnation, others stories had a moral. I liked the latter. We would all discuss the type of sermon the priest preached, we came from different areas of the city and whoever had the priest with the best stories, there we would go. When we got home the first thing Mammy would ask was, "Which church did you go to do your mission?" You could not tell a lie and say you went if you did not go, she could see your guilt and knew you had lied, so we went. The reason I was with Daddy on this occasion was because I had tried another church and thought the priest was too severe so I was testing the waters so to speak.

Daddy continued quoting to me on our walk to the Jesuit church, "an educated man is an educated individual; an educated woman is an educated family." I did go back to school when I travelled. I realised that a better education meant a better job. When my father died, my sister was in Hong Kong. News of my father's death was in the obituary column in China and Hong Kong newspapers. I am sure he would have been honoured as he travelled the world in his books and in his mind's eye. It is only right and fitting that tribute should be paid to him around the world.

Chapter 15

Daddy's Garden

Daddy's garden was very well kept with beautiful flowers. Even though we had a large family, we respected his garden and did not abuse it. He spent hours working the soil, attending to his roses and reading books on gardening.

Whenever he saw a plant he admired in a garden in the countryside when he was doing electrical work there, if he did not have the plant, in conversation with the owner, he would admire the plant and the owner would be very happy with a fellow gardening enthusiast, he would be offered a cutting after much discussion about plants in general. He was well versed on flowers and plants and knew many of the Latin names for plants. Later in his life he planted more perennials then flowers as they were less work and not as expensive to buy.

There was a high wall at the front of our garden, along the entire wall there were rose bushes with a perfusion of beautiful pink roses; they lasted most of the summer. When they were in bud they were deep pink and when opened a lighter pink.

When I go to the Chelsea flower show I look at the roses, I cannot find the perfection I found in Daddy's pink rose. His garden had other roses in it, deep yellow roses and one of the red roses was red velvet in colour, it was too heavy for the stem and its perfume was so strong and intoxicating. He showed me how he grafted a rose tree; he worked like a surgeon, making an incision into the tree grafting the new cutting at an angle, after treating it with a fertilising powder. He bound it up and he explaining as he went step by step.

There were other flowers: Gladioli, tulips, pansies, marigold and many others. When he wanted manure he would look at his roses wistfully and say "If I had some cow manure it would work a treat on my roses "off I would go without another word. I would be the only one of his children to go to the field with a bucket and coal shovels where the cows were happily chewing the cud. I would fill my bucket with cow dung and bring it back for him. He hummed a tune as he busily worked the manure into the soil saying, "It's a bit late in the year for the manure they might turn the leaves yellow."

One day I was in town getting some shopping for Mammy and passed a flower shop, I saw gladioli in the window at two shillings and sixpence that is half a crown each, a great deal of money at that time. Large houses in Limerick would have a display sat in there fire place in the summer months or in a Waterford crystal vase on their highly polished tables in their dining room.

Now mid-week Mammy would be complaining that she did not know how she would manage until Friday payday. She complained regularly but always managed. I did not think of that at the time. As I passed a flower shop in town I saw a large vase of gladioli through the window. I had a brain flash I went in to the flower shop and asked for the lady in charge. I said, "My father has a nursery. He sent me to ask, if you need some gladioli?" The manager said, "Yes, but I could only pay one shilling and threepence, you understand. I have my overheads." I continued with "how many would you like?" She answered, "As many as you can bring me, but they must be in bud, "I said. "I will let my father know."

I hurried back home and told my Mammy. She was worried that they would be missed by Daddy but she could not pass the chance of a little more income midweek. I decided to pick a large bunch of flowers for the aunts in Pery Square. I returned to the shop with seven gladioli and got the money. The lady in the shop was very happy with her purchase and I was elated with the transaction.

I carried on my journey to Pery Square and my aunts were overjoyed with their large bunch of flowers, a gift from my Daddy's garden. There were many ooo's and aaa's as they displayed the flowers around the house. Mammy had given me instructions to come straight home after I had given the flowers to my aunts. I told them I could not stay as I had to get the dinner for Mammy. Normally I would stay and help them.

When Daddy came home for his dinner, he said, "Marie, did you bring flowers to Pery square?" I told him, "I did Daddy." "Did they like them?" I said, "They did." He asked, "Where did they display them?" The house was very large. I said, "In the hall and on the other floors upstairs" which was not a lie. He was very happy that I should bring the flowers to my Aunts. I should have gone into the sales business in later life as I loved the negotiations and got a real buzz out of doing a business transaction.

Years later after my Mammy passed away I told Daddy. I thought he would be proud to know that his flowers were of a superior quality and sold in one of Limericks finer flower shops. He gave me a quizzical look and said "Did you Marie "I said "yes"

Chapter 16

My Daddy's Sister Margaret

My Daddy would note I had an idle day and say go and visit your aunts at Pery House and give them a hand. So off I would go into town and up to Pery Square. My hand would go into the letter box. And I would pull out the key and open the door. The hall was large and square, with many doors. One of my aunts would appear from behind a door. Aunty Monica with her little dog would be going out for a walk in the People's park in Pery Square doing their constitutional among the beautifully-kept flower beds that changed with the seasons. There was also a bandstand that on a hot day would have a brass band playing that made the park come alive. The pavilion had circular seating, if I close my eyes, I can still see my Aunty Maggie sitting there looking like Ms Marple acted by Joan Hicks or should I say Ms Marple looked like her. She was dressed in the same style, a coat of soft grey cloth, a silk blouse and grey skirt. Her long, soft grey hair was brushed into a bun at the back of her head and she wore a grey hat and highly polished brown laced court shoes.

Aunty Margaret was autistic but not diagnosed as such. When she was young she would be labelled as odd and left at that. She was brought up in Ennis at my grandfather's farm called Cappahard. As the elders died she moved to Pery House to live with her family. She came and went at her leisure. She was on time for all her meals and attended church twice a day. In the evening she could be seen in the back sitting room. In the background the radio played classical music or a play. I could not tell you if she listened or not as her facial expressions were hard to read and she had a shy look and did not have eye contact with anyone. I was always sorry that I had not asked her questions to unlock her story. I think we left her to her world and she seemed happy. She never got any of our names correct they were all pronounced differently.

She never looked at you or directed any questions at you; it was rather said as a statement or thrown out in the air. When I visited on my return from England one year, one of my aunts asked me to answer the bell to the front door, which was on the first floor. As I was about to go upstairs, my Aunty Margaret came out from an anteroom off the kitchen and went up the stairs before me. She said, "If the Pope came to visit, they would give him a job to do." That was the first coherent statement I had ever heard from her. If the aunties had any private family business to discuss they would check that she was not in one of the small rooms attached to the kitchen. She would sometimes be brushing her hair getting ready to go out.

The problem was she could not tell a lie and if she was asked a direct question she would tell the truth. If it was confidential it was better that she did not know. They were a very private family. My Aunt Maggie would ask me if I would like a pot of tea. I was warned to say no to her as her sisters were worried about the quantity of pots of tea she drank. They would make tea when she went on her way. However she lived a long and healthy life and towards the end all she wanted was bread and butter and a pot of tea.

Chapter 17

Corbally

I tried to show that I had settled down after arriving home with Mammy. The next day was sunny and my younger sister was preparing to go swimming to Corbally swimming baths. I said to Mammy I would go with her. Mammy was quite happy that I seemed to be settling down once more in Limerick. My sister called in to her friend's house on our road. I took the opportunity to head off in the direction of Corbally. When I got as far as King John's Castle I headed to Granny's house

I will digress here and fill you in on what it was like on a hot summer's day in my childhood. We would go to Corbally throughout the hot summer days to swim. After dinner we would gather our swimming gear and meet friends on the road or knock on doors to call for them.

Then we walked about three miles. We relied on our legs as our transport, along Farranshone over the Shannon River past King John's Castle across Nicholas Street and out on the road to Corbally where I would meet with friends.

The walk down Corbally Road was the most pleasant. I remember very hot days, passing a very large tree with so many birds all twittering and making so much noise. I would come to a wooden door, to what; I referred to it as a secret garden. I would peep in the flap of the letter box, to a beautiful lawn, immaculately kept, with a tennis court and a large cottage with many flowers in front. I used to think when I grew up I would have a house just like that. It has not happened yet.

Then on down the road, feeling it was getting very hot and longing to immerse myself in the cold water of the river Shannon.

I would linger outside a house on my walk down the country road, set back in what resembled an English country garden, an ancient concrete path leading up to the front door. I was drawn to this property with the garden of hollyhocks and roses, flowers of blue and lavender. I know this house from somewhere in my memory and I longed to enter it. I had a picture in my mind of me as a very young baby on a blanket on the bed, the curtains fluttering in the gentle summer breeze. In the bay window sat a kidney-shaped dressing table in white, drawers on both sides and a gathered curtain of roses covering the centre between the outer drawers. Light filtered in and dancing in rainbow colours off a crystal bowl, there was a silver set of brush, comb and mirror, lying on the dressing table. A golden light lit up the trellis of large pink roses and green leaves on the wall paper. I had heard that my aunt and uncle rented a property on this road when they were first married. I was never told what property. This house is the keeper of my dream.

When I arrived at the gate leading to the bathing area, there was a drive going down to the river. There were around eight changing rooms and a little children's paddling pool. At the side of the river was the pool edge with sandstone colour tiles, then the other side of the river was the same. You had to be a strong swimmer to make it across. It was not so far, but most of us were not strong swimmers.

When I was younger I would go under the bridge to swim. It was further down the river, or, I would pretend to swim. I would have one foot on the ground and it took some time before I could swim properly. The water was not as deep there as in the pool area. There were children swimming in the river, teenagers lounging on the grass, hoping for a tan, adults walking their dogs, parents with their families, people passing through on their walks.

I loved the walk from the bridge along a narrow shaded path, a stream running down along one side, with trees high in the sky. The sun sent shards of light filtering through the leaves, light and shadow dancing in patterns along the pathway. Beyond the trees a strip of land on the other side, stretched to the water's edge, to meet the river Shannon on its way to Ardnacrusha. The path ended where the river widened to reveal many beautiful swans. It always reminded me of the story of *The Wild Swans*, a fairy story by Hans Christian Andersen. It is about a princess who rescued her eleven brothers from a spell cast by an evil queen, I liked to think they could turn back when they wanted to, as they loved this spot on the river Shannon and there were so many swans there. The scenery everywhere you turned was perfection: hills, mountains and remnants of round towers. We accepted it as our right, that moment when the beauty of the scenery, peace and solitude pulled together; it heightens your powers of observation and imagination.

When I eventually learned to swim I graduated from the bridge to the pool. That was where the teenagers hung out. There were a group of bigger girls looking very glamorous in sun glasses and revealing swimsuits. They talked to the big boys.

I loved swimming. We would be in and out of the river all afternoon with friends and at about five o' clock we would make our way home starving. The saying I could eat a horse was mentioned on more than one occasion. We would go home a different route along the river on a narrow path looking at the reeds and the blue irises growing in between them. We would watch motionless fish basking in the clear waters of the Shannon.

I walked on to Grannie's. My aunt and her family lived with her. I told them what my Daddy said and I told them I was going back. My aunt did not think it was a good idea to go by train and boat as my Daddy would be working in that area. It was decided that I should go by plane. Granny went upstairs and brought down the money and my birth certificate. She gave me the rest of the fare to travel back by the six o' clock plane. My aunt came to the airport with me by taxi.

As I looked out the taxi window, I remembered my first visit to Shannon Airport. Mammy said, "We are going to say goodbye to your Daddy's niece and her children. Her husband has gone ahead to prepare the way, they are immigrating to America." I was very excited as I had never been to Shannon Airport before. I would see the planes land and take off, flying to and from foreign countries. We motored along to a scenic view out from the Ennis road past Bunratty Castle. A fortress was there in 1251 before a stone castle was built in 1277. The present castle was built in 1425. Dirty Nelly's, a famous watering hole (pub), is alongside. People would stop on their journey to or from the airport, Ennis or further afield, to partake of some refreshments.

Daddy told us a story about his family; they had a farm in Ennis and a house in Limerick city. Travelling on their journeys to the city, the ladies of the house had their own pony and trap, but as their pony had a loose shoe they decided to use the horse that the uncles had. The horse was so accustomed to pulling in at Dirty Nelly's while the uncles had a pint or two of Guinness. When the horse got as far as Dirty Nelly's he pulled in and would go no further, to the dismay of Daddy's aunt. They had no option but to order tea and wait until the horse was ready to resume his journey. They, like the Queen, were not amused. Daddy chuckled as he recalled this memory.

My journey to the airport was an adventure looking out the window of the car enjoying the scenery. We arrived and were greeted by a mixture of family and friends in the departure lounge. Aunts, uncles and cousins tried to converse in a light and jolly tone. They talked about the weather and the oncoming mission week at all the churches in Limerick. Everyone was required to attend.

Daddy's niece's name was Mary. She was my Uncle Dominic's daughter and had five young children, two girls in pretty dresses and three boys. The boys had their hair cut short in case they would not be able to locate a barber immediately when they arrived in the States. They wore grey suits. Their short pants looked a size too big for them, but would have to last them for some time. Inside their jackets they wore Fair Isle short sleeved jumpers. They looked a little lost and confused.

Everyone looked with sadness at the young mother and her children they worried about her coping with her new surroundings in a foreign country without the support of the extended family. Being there at the airport, to see her off on her journey, could be likened to a wake. We were engulfed in sadness and loneliness, trying to lighten the mood in our farewells. Mary was holding the baby and the four children stood like steps of stairs at her side. The time came to say our goodbyes and the family and friends discreetly moved a little way back to allow the parents to bid a last farewell, to their daughter and grandchildren. To share this last moment together there was a tear in every eye. Mary said she would come back to see them as soon as she could. Her mother cried and said she may not be here when she returned.

Mary went on to have more children it was many years before she was able to return as a middle-aged woman and an American, on a holiday one summer's day.

The last I remember was the little children following their Mammy holding on to the rail making their way steadily up the steep steps leading on to the plane. A last wave goodbye at the top of the steps and they were swallowed up in the large silver bird. Then up, up and away they went. Another family leaving home, going where the work was, to seek a living, provide for their growing family and hopefully have a better life in a faraway land.

At the airport now it was my turn. My aunt bade me farewell. wished me every success and happiness in my new life. As I went in through the departure lounge my last sight was of her smiling and waving with tears in her eyes.

I returned to England. I had a friend, Peggy who was married to a friend of John's. John and Peggy had a discussion and it was decided that if we were married my mother could not bring me home again.

John and I went for a walk. He led me into a travel agent, booked two tickets to Gretna Green and that was the marriage proposal. We arrived in Gretna Green after a journey of eight hours by train. It seemed an eternity. I cannot say I was worried about where I would stay. I was in a bit of a haze or naïve.

We made enquiries for lodging in the area. We were not the first couple to come to Gretna Green. The locals knew where there were lodgings and they gave us directions. The lady of the house told us they had no more rooms left in the house, however there was a caravan and if we were willing to share it with another couple we were welcome.

So we stayed in a caravan in the back of a house where the lady rented rooms to couples waiting to get married in Gretna Green. There were six couples, four couples living in the house and two couples in the caravan.

Chapter 18

Waiting On Marriage

We shared a caravan with a German couple, Hans and Gertie. We became friends, they agreed to be our witnesses and we agreed to be theirs. We had to live in Scotland for three weeks before we registered with the registrar's office to get married and then seven days' wait. It was a long wait and we had arguments over little things. I think it was me more than John. The strain of waiting. I had an underlying worry that this was just a legal contract and not a proper marriage.

Life was not all bad; the men borrowed fishing rods and we all went fishing. The only thing they caught were eels. It rained a lot. We sat around the small table in the caravan and we talked about a wide range of subjects. They told us in Germany the woman could not get married until twenty-one and the man not until twenty-five without their parents' consent. Of the six couples waiting to get married a good number of them were German. I asked Hans if his father was in the war in Germany. He said he was in the regular army. If he did not join he would be shot.

A large van which was a mobile shop stopped at our village regularly. The man pulled down small steps and we could go inside and make our purchases. It was stacked with all you would need. We would get fruit, toothpaste and biscuits if needed.

We took a trip to Carlisle once. A man was talking loudly on the bus, he may have had drink taken. The bus was on a long country road. When we came to a bus stop the conductor got off. She must have made a phone call at a telephone box, (no mobile phones in those days) because when we got to the next stop a police car was waiting to take him off. Now that I think about it he could have been racist about John and I being together because he was looking in our direction. I did not understand what he was saying. His accent was very strong. I think John knew. It was not his habit to comment, after all we were emigrants and it was not our country. Sunday was a total shutdown: no shops, pubs, or restaurant opened not that we went in to a pub.

The time got near I supposed I panicked. We had many arguments, I don't recall what about. Little things I suppose. I was broody. When I thought about a wedding, it was of a church wedding with bells ringing out the good news. Happy smiling faces; the glow of soft candlelight around the altar; bridesmaids in their fine clothes of lilacs or pink. I had it all worked out in my mind.

There would be heightened anticipation as the wedding procession moved down the aisle. First to come would be my mother, as the mother of the bride. Radiant in her attire, hat sat pertly on her head, glowing with pride. Then the page boys followed by flower girls and bridesmaids. I on my father's arm, his precious gift, to give wrapped in a gown and veil of white. The wedding party would fill the church with love, a warm and fuzzy feeling. Smiles and tears, beaming faces, heartfelt good wishes to guide us safely on our way. John with his entourage standing to attention at the altar side, waiting to greet me as his bride. A moment frozen in time, a glimmer of love, pride and joy to be remembered. A friendly priest, a kind and cheerful man. A wedding to be celebrated in an ancient church. John and I trusting in one another, a new family in the making. A wedding song to fill the rafters of the church. A bit of a do, a celebration, togetherness, a united front. A happy and glorious wedding.

One has to remember I was young and believed in fairy tales. I thought all would be lost if I got married in a register office, with no family or friends to wish us well.

I said I was not getting married on the day before the wedding. I got the bus to the station. The next train to London was about three hours away. I sat in the empty silent station. Nothing moved. I was suspended in space with time to contemplate, to go over what I would do when I got to London. Now in the cold light of reality, I had to forget the fairy tale wedding. I had to see things as they were. My sister could not help me as she was also pregnant and in the same situation. I went over and over every aspect in my brain. My emotions flowed and rushed like a river's torrent, trying to escape between the rocks. Wedding blessings, to me, meant blessed and authorised by the church. I did not recognise a marriage in a registry office. It was not how I was brought up. I wanted to have my family and friends all smiling with approval and blessings. I wanted the dream, happy ever after. I wanted them to be proud of John and me.

I was never one who could communicate how I felt. John and I were cut from the same cloth. We loved one another but never spoke about it. I could talk forever: stories, news, that is without communicating on a deeper level. So as the wedding date loomed without reassurance from John. I felt very insecure and upset without anyone to discuss my feelings with. I had to brood and go over in my mind, analysing and reanalysing, what the future held.

John came to England to help his family. He did not plan on me. He did not come to Britain for himself. In his mind he had made promises to his mother, to repay his passage money and to help his family. The commitment to a young wife and baby was not his to make but he made it. He was going to stick to it. He was an honourable young man who wanted to do right by everyone.

I would go back to our room in Ladbroke Grove. I could not ask for help from the Welfare. If I did not have money or a place, the Welfare may take my baby away and tell me to get a job to keep myself. After reanalysing the facts, John looked very good to me. I was looked after and safe with him and I could not consider any other man. So I picked up my case and went back. I do not recall having any money other than a few shillings. I was like the Queen, John carried the money. When I entered the caravan, Hans, Gertie and John made no comment. I said to John, that I would go back to London with him but not to get married. I was too proud to say "I had come back" in case he did not want to marry me. I had embarrassed him. I did not know how he would take it. The hour was late so we retired to bed. In the morning I was still in bed. Everyone was getting dressed in their wedding outfits and getting ready to go to the register office to get married. John was dressed in his suit. He said to me that I had to get up after promising to be Hans and Gertie's witness. I got up and got ready. I put on my grey suit and little hat, took my gloves and little bag. That was my wedding outfit. As we walked up the hill to the register office the other couples joked with John and said, "Have you got the ring, John?" He said, "What ring?" We all stood in the hall waiting to be called in as couples to be married. We were called in alphabetical order and John's surname started with C so we were the first to be called. He placed his hand at my back and ushered me into a large room with a woman behind a desk. The wedding took five minutes. I was disappointed that there were no prayers. It went: 'Do you take this man/woman...?' A sentence by the registrar and we were done. Next couple. I was happy that the decision was made, no more analysing and dissecting in my brain. I was Mrs C. John was my husband and I would be a good wife. The best ever. There were photographers and newspaperman outside the register office to greet us. They asked John and me for a story. John said "no." He never mentioned me leaving the day before my wedding, at that time or during the rest of our lives.

Chapter 19

Married Life

We went back to the caravan, gathered our belongings together, picked up our cases, said our goodbyes and headed off to the train station. Hans and Gertie had nowhere to stay when we arrived in London, so John said to stay with us. They were very grateful; they had no money left to pay for a hotel. They would have to stay at the station until the following day. There was no food left on the train. We had a very long journey but the catering staff managed to get us soup at one of the stops. When we arrived back at Ladbroke Grove, we stopped at a fish and chip shop near the station and the man sold us some bread and butter as well.

We only had one bed in the room; a gas cooker; a cupboard to put our food in and mice who shared ownership of the room. The house was condemned and we were looking for a room somewhere else. We would look at the noticeboards; they made interesting reading. 'No coloured need apply'. Then the *piece de resistance* was when one read: No children; no coloured; no cats; no dogs AND NO IRISH NEED APPLY'. John laughed. He said, "They have included you now." Gertie ate very well and then was sick all night. We showed them the sights of London including Trafalgar Square with the pigeons. Every visitor went there in the Sixties and Seventies. We saw them off from Victoria Station the next day. We never saw or heard of them again.

Chapter 20

Portobello Road

On a Saturday morning John and I would go to Portobello Road. It was always the bubbling, busy place, it is today. We would mingle with the crowds walking from Notting Hill Gate, south to north down Portobello Road.

On a sunny Saturday morning, there was a holiday atmosphere in the air. It was full of sounds, colours, sunlight and life. The stallholders with their Cockney slang, music, movement of carts, voices from the four corners of the globe, locals, visitors, tourists. Stalls were filled in pyramids of colourful tropical vegetables and fruits, apples and pears, seasonal vegetables.

We meandered on the path, hemmed in by shops and stalls or moved to the middle of the road, to view rails of new, vintage and second-hand clothes. There were goods from the East, brass items shining like gold, beads and the tinkling of bells, the air was filled with music, Indian carpets and prayer rugs. It was the scent of India: curry and spices.

There were hot dogs and beef burgers with buns. The smell of food made your mouth water: Cockles and mussels in vinegar. jellied eels in pots; stalls with fine bone china and crystal; stalls laden with silver spoons; tea and coffee sets; silver frames; antique shops to search for a special gift, to gaze at an Aladdin's cave of treasures; paintings by artists, good and not so good; porcelain figurines and plates; books, books, books. We would linger to hear a performer playing, on the pavement. Sometimes it would be an Irish fiddler or a Scotsman playing his bagpipes, a steel band, or a juggler performing his art. There would always be an artist to draw your portrait.

We would stand outside the Electric Cinema to see the latest release showing that week. The Irish music would take me back to Limerick and be a reminder of standing outside Woolworth's, ice cream in hand, on a Saturday afternoon listening to three blind fiddlers playing traditional music, John would buy the chicken and fruit for Sunday's dinner and I would chose some flowers from a colourful flower stall and a stick of hot fresh bread from the bakery. We would make our way home, our senses filled with sights and sounds to satisfy us and to see us through the working week.

Chapter 21

Phillis's Marriage

After we were married. I was nervous about writing to Mammy and letting my family know about my marriage and me expecting a baby, in case I had another visit from Mammy and there were more problems. I discussed this with Phillis saying, "How are we going to tell them?" She said, "Leave it to me, I have to tell them I got married to David. I will write home and let them know." Phillis married David, her fiancé, in a Catholic church in Queensway.

One morning we made our way to a church in Queensway. We entered by the side door and made our way up the aisle. The sound of our high-heeled shoes echoed in the stillness of the church which was empty but for the four of us and the priest. John and I were the best man and maid of honour. The light shone through the stained glass window, at the back of the altar, while the priest conducted the marriage ceremony. When the priest came to the traditional rites of marriage he said, "With this ring I thee wed, this gold and silver I thee give." Phillis looked at the plate; it just held the gold wedding ring, no silver. She turned to John and asked, "Have you got any silver?" He dug his hand into his pocket to reveal a collection of coins. He went for a sixpence. I quickly dipped my hand in and took a half a crown and put it on the plate with the gold ring. When we left the church, John said, "That is the last I will see of that silver." We all laughed and returned to Phillis's small flat where she had cooked dinner for us. Money was short and a proper wedding reception was not on the cards.

Phillis wrote to my parents to say that we were both married and expecting babies. My mother wrote to Phillis. I did not see her reply. I got a rubber squeaky doll sitting on a potty from my father in the post. I kept it for many years. It was a very kind thing to do and I was delighted. Daddy was happy with becoming a grandfather though he would have been happier if it had been under different circumstances.

I settled down to married life. The bath in our house was unusable. We went to the public baths. It was heaven, a large bath, as much hot water as you wanted, for a shilling you could get a towel, shampoo and soap. If the water got lukewarm you could add more hot water. These are little things but when you have nothing it is pure luxury. On one of our excursions to the baths, we met a friend of John's. We stopped for a chat and a soft rain started to fall. John asked, "What are those white bubbles coming from your hair?" He had thick, black, wavy hair. He said, "They gave me a hair product and I put it in my hair after I dried it." We laughed; it was shampoo. John said, "Boy, you wash your hair with it, it is shampoo not Brylcreem."

Once a week I would go to the baths to wash my clothes. They had a very large laundry. I had heard you could do your laundry there. I went in with a large laundry bag, sheets, pillowcases and our clothes. There was a little office where you paid, it was sixpence an hour. It also had a small canteen where you could buy a hot pie and tea. The entrance was through large doors and there in front of me was a large industrial laundry. I stood looking lost and amazed. An older English lady asked if I needed help. She said, "You all right, my love?" She led me to a double stone sink, next to her. She showed me how to use it. One sink was to wash your clothes and the other was to boil the clothes. It had an element somewhere in the sink that boiled the water. When you finished washing your white cloths, sheets, pillow cases, shirts, you could transfer them into the other sink and boil them. She said that she did her young men's shirts. I realised it was a job for her. She had clients for whom she did the laundry. It had large industrial driers and after wringing the clothes in a smaller machine, then into the drier they went. While my clothes were drying I could get a cup of tea and the pie. Then on to the ironing room with lines of ironing boards and irons wired to the ceiling. I ironed all my clothes and brought them home and placed them neatly in the drawers.

One day I came back home to find my room door opened and the lock broken. Someone had broken into our room. The watch my father gave me had been stolen. The gas meter was broken into. I had a savings box containing half a crown coins. This was to put towards a cot for my baby; also John's post office savings book was gone. The drawers were emptied, clothes scattered around and the place was a mess. I was very upset about my watch. For many years afterwards, John asked if I would like a watch for Christmas. I said no because the watch given by my father was special to me.

Chapter 22

My Friend's Baby

We continued to look for a room as we had to move before the baby was born. I took up knitting. I had knitted before so I knew how. I would buy two or three balls of wool out of money saved from the grocery money. The wool was in all the pastel colours except pink and blue. I knitted cardigans, hats, mitts, bootees, layettes, white shawl and layette for the christening.

My friend Peggy had a little boy, his father was West Indian and Peggy was English. When I finished knitting I would go over to see her and her baby. I put the garment up to his little face to see if the colour suited him. I knew that if it looked good on her baby it would look lovely on mine.

On one occasion, Peggy was cooking dinner at a cooker situated in the hall upstairs. I said hello and passed her to go in to her room to see her baby boy. There was no baby in the cot or room I came out and asked Peggy where the baby was. She turned off the cooker and came to look. She said, "Oh God, oh God, I left him outside the shop." We took off at top speed racing up Westbourne grove to Portobello road, me in my rather large condition running around people, weaving in and out to save time. We got to the shop and there he was asleep in his pram. We were so relieved to find him safe. Peggy asked me not to mention it to John or her husband. I learned a good lesson, when I had my baby, I would not go inside a shop that I could not bring the pushchair into. There is no way I would leave any of my children outside a shop.

I was booked into St Mary Abbot Hospital, Kensington to give birth. I would travel there by train to see the doctor. I loved to walk up, Kensington high road and look at the shop windows. I never went in as it did not occur to me to go inside and look around, if I was not buying anything. Now people go into shops, wander around and browse. They don't intend to purchase unless they see something they really like. Maybe it is the difference with having money or having none.

I was putting on a lot of weight and my doctor asked me what I was eating. I told him and he said that that couldn't put on that kind of weight: four pounds in two weeks. He said try again, as a last resort I said my husband made me a tonic. He wanted to know what the tonic was. I told him it was Guinness, eggs, sweetened milk and what else I do not know. The doctor said only I was putting the weight on, not the baby. I was very unhappy as I walked from the hospital down the Kensington high street. I was hungry. I had left my room early in the morning and now I was feeling guilty about my weight and upset. So the only comfort was to pop into the next Wimpy café I could see on the high road and have a feed of fried eggs, burger beans and chips and waddle home content.

Chapter 23

Visit From The Priest

John had gone to work on the night shift. He started at seven o'clock. I was alone and heavily pregnant, when there was a knock on the door. I opened to see a priest, middle-aged and unsmiling. He informed me that my aunt and godmother had written to him and asked him to come and see me. I sat down on the bed in shock. I offered him a seat but he declined. His oppressive stance sucked all good will from the room. I started to scan the room worriedly. There was no pattern on the lino as my landlord was very mean. He bought the cheapest he could get from Portobello Road and carried it home on his shoulders. When I washed the floor the pattern came off. There was an old cooker used by many people over the years. The landlord would have bought it second hand in the first place. It was in a corner of the room. A small table covered in oil cloth and two chairs sat against the wall. I was very concerned as to how it would look to him.

He fired a series of questions at me and after hearing I got married in a register office he said, "Do you know that you could get a divorce? You would be eligible to get married in a church one day." I didn't answer. I kept my head bowed as I did not want him to see what I was thinking. He offered no assistance or words of comfort. He, at least, had the good grace not to tell me to put my child up for adoption or I missed that part. I opted out of this conversation. The inference was there.

I did not mention it to John; he would not understand why I still went to the church. I always felt that religion was a matter of faith and not the administrators of that faith. I was so upset. He had the ear of the Irish community, some were very successful, they invested in properties, they rented out flats and rooms. He could have asked around if there were any flats to rent or even a better room. He did not choose to do so.

At that time the Irish stayed in their own community, like all emigrants. They felt safer together. They got support from one another. Even though they were immigrants they could be prejudiced against people of a different colour or different race. The priest could have put in a good word for me, but did not. Did he think I was beyond redemption? He left me feeling empty and alone. Little did he know, given the same set of circumstances, I would do the same again.

I never saw him again for which I am eternally grateful. I knew he had fulfilled his duty to my aunt and reported back to her. His responsibilities ended there. He had located me, I was not dead and maybe I was lost to his version of the church. As he left, my eyes scanned the room once more, now I saw it as he would have, I was overcome with a sense of shame that my room was not sparkling and inviting. Maybe he would have sat down and had a cup of tea if it was a more desirable property. Approval is something I have to talk about here; we all need it in our lives. Do we rely too much on the approval of our fellow man? How do we react to negative approval? Is it worse when it is dispensed by family or priest? Does positive approval encourage us to soar to the greatest heights or can negative approval encourage us to make bad decisions and sink to the lowest depths? Is approval a measuring stick by which we measure ourselves? Is it stronger within a group, small town, or a village? Are we ruled by our need to be approved by the tribe, village, town, city, country, priest or world? Is being unique and different not acceptable?

Chapter 24

Eviction

When I first moved into Camelford Road there was a family from Pakistan living across the road from me: father, grandfather and five children aged from eleven down to one. The father went from door to door selling out of a suitcase; table cloths, bedspreads chair back covers etc . . .The children were watching me for some time, I would smile and say hello. One day the little group of four children approached me, the two older girls pushing forward the younger brother, to talk to me. He was shy but he managed to say, "They want to know your name." I told them "Marie" and smiled. From then on the ice was broken. When I was on the road coming back from the shops, they would talk to me. One day I made an apple pie for them and asked them if they would like some. They came into my room huddled together. I offered the pie on little plates, again the girls pushed the brother forward to ask the question "Was it pig?" I told them that it was fruit. They were quiet happy with that.

Grandfather was very old; he sat on a rug, a hubble bubble pipe in the corner, his Quran opened on his lap. Either the eleven-year-old or the eight-year-old would carry the baby on their hip. I was invited to their flat. The eleven-year-old did all the work. She kneaded the flour for chapattis like an expert. I asked the grandfather "Where is the children's mother". He told me that their father's first wife died in childbirth, giving birth to the eldest girl and the father married again. The other children were from the second wife. She was not happy in England and wanted to go home. He told her it meant divorce, she agreed. They divorced and she returned to her country, leaving the children with their father and grandfather.

One day as I was coming up Camelford Road, I saw that all of my neighbour's goods: paraffin fire, pots, crockery, everything was being thrown out of their upstairs window by two bulky men. They were working for Peter Rachman, a racketeer landlord who was notorious for his exploitation of his rental tenants. He reigned in the Fifties to the early Sixties, in the Notting hill area. They were being evicted. The grandfather was distressed and sitting on some items he had retrieved. Nobody called the police. The father asked me to take the baby and adopt her. I could not because I was heavily pregnant, eighteen-years-old and John and I had to find a place to live.

There were some ladies who lived in a house on our street. Their occupation could be called into question. They showed great kindness to the family. They cleared the basement in their house and gave it to the family. The next day I went to buy milk from the corner shop. There was an Italian lady I recognised from the street. She was in her late 30s and comely in appearance.

She was carrying a beautiful baby. I did not remember seeing her pregnant. I would have noticed as I was pregnant. I said to her, "I did not know you had a baby, she is beautiful." The baby was dressed in a lemon knitted cardigan and a pretty dress. She had dark hair and eyes and looked Italian. She said, "It is the Pakistani baby. We are adopting her. When the papers are through we will leave this road and buy a house ".

While we lived in the Grove, I heard talk of racism. I did not see much of it. On one occasion John and I went into a bar. There was a singer on a little stage, when he saw us come in he looked at us and changed his song to a song, which I knew well and got his meaning *"If I were a blackbird I would whistle and sing."* It was an Irish pub. We did not stay. On another occasion three Irishmen saw me walking with John in Ladbroke Grove. One caught me as we passed and swung me around, when he put me down, I lost it and said, "It is people like you who make me ashamed to be Irish "All three apologised. I did not go to bars or dances where we would meet trouble.

In Ladbroke Grove there was a cosmopolitan community: European, Caribbean and African mostly. Now I could look around Ladbroke Grove and Notting Hill and see the community I lived in. Some white women married emigrants from the West Indies and other countries. Inter-marriage was now beginning to be looked at, as if the women were not decent women. Some were not from the best families or some were not the best of men or women, which happens in all races. Because of the difference in colour inter-married couples came under more scrutiny.

When money is scarce in the family, young men like John are the first to be sent abroad for education and work. Some men sent for their wives and children or girlfriends, as soon as they could save the fare and get a place for them to live. They were all lonely, missed their Caribbean islands in the sun, with good fruit, fish and good food, friendly neighbours who knew, who they were, who knew their grandparents and family history. They came from villages and towns where they belonged, where you respected the lady who had little but her religion and the man who worked hard and provided for his family. Some emigrants got into relationships and made a life with their partners or wives and started a family.

People born in the UK had no concept of what life was like in the Caribbean. Now with travel being affordable to all, the world is a smaller place. It would have been hard for them, in the Sixties to look past colour and see the same structure in their population, of wealth, education and class, as in a small island. It is the same as every nation of the world.

All who came as emigrants did not have success stories but there were thousands that did. I believe the ones that made good would have made good, had they stayed in their own backyard. The opportunities offered to those who travelled and those who took those opportunities up and worked hard, were some of the success stories.

Some failed. They took to drink to numb the pain of loneliness, poor housing, hard work with little pay for long hours and some because they took a liking to drink. Some had poor health and some would never succeed, no matter what country they lived in. That was the way of all emigrants no matter where they came from.

Small islands and poor countries did not have the economic advancement or job opportunities that the UK, USA and Canada offered. After the war they had a shortage of workers due to the loss of men in the First and Second World Wars, so they advertised in Barbados for bus drivers. They offered training for Caribbean and Irish nurses. They needed people from India, Bangladesh and Pakistan for the textile and steel mills in Lancashire and Yorkshire. Then there were the people who just travelled to improve their situation. These are just a few examples of the flow of emigration in the late Fifties and Sixties to the UK.

Chapter 25

My Daughter's Birth

John was working nights and my time to give birth was overdue, so it was decided that I would stay with my sister and her husband, I went into labour but it was a false alarm and the next day I went home to Ladbroke Grove. John was looking for a room in Harlesden which he found in St Mary's Road as there was a compulsory purchase order on the house we lived in, on Camelford Road in Ladbroke Grove. The houses on the road have been demolished since then. The road no longer exists as it was, there are blocks of flats there now, we had no chance of re-housing with the council as it went on a points system: disabilities, how many children you had, etc. so John had to look for a room.

That Saturday we moved to St Mary's Road in Harlesden, I had a show but did not tell John as I'd had a false alarm a few days before. On the Monday I went for a check up to the hospital and they kept me in. I had started contractions.

When John came to the hospital I was near to having my baby but I did not realise it. John looked very ill and I told him to go to work as it was getting near his starting time. Phillis said he did not go to work. He went home and was very sick.

I had a baby girl at seven thirty in the evening. They showed me the baby; she was all squashed up as all newborn babies are when they come out of the womb. I thought how could I have such an ugly baby and went off to sleep. I was probably out of it by then. The last thing I remember was the doctor saying, "I think she has jaundice." I said "No. she has not, her dad is Indian." She probably had a touch of jaundice, as most newborn babies have.

In the middle of the night I woke up. I looked around to see a large ward with eight beds on each side. The mothers were sleeping. I looked for my baby, but there was no sign. Most of the babies were taken to the nursery at night, to give the mothers a good night's rest. I got up and went to the nursery, the door was shut, so I stood outside. I was afraid if I went in, the nurse would tell me off. After what seemed a long time I returned to my bed.

I waited until morning when the nurses arrived on the ward. It was a hive of activity. I sat on the bed and watched. They were wheeling the babies from the nursery to the mothers. They did not bring my baby. I drew the attention of one of the nurses. I told her that I'd had a baby last night. She said, "Are you sure? There are no more babies in the nursery; maybe she is still in the doctor's room after he examined her last night." I followed her not leaving anything to chance. There she was fast asleep on her own. I wheeled her back to my bed.

I took her into the bed with me. She was the most beautiful baby I had ever seen. I kept looking at her, her beautiful brown eyes with long eye lashes, her pencil eyebrows, cupid lips, coffee peaches and cream complete with black waves of hair covering her skull like a cap, a little circular shape around the back of her beautiful head.

The nurse came to see me. She said, "Your husband is outside the ward. I will let him in when the mothers have finished feeding their babies and they are settled down." All the babies were settled in their cots and as a special privilege, as John had to work nights; he was allowed in to see me and the baby. He walked down the middle of the ward, the centre of attention, with all the mothers sitting up in their beds looking at him. He glanced into the cot to see his daughter as he went past. I was sad that he did not pick her up and see her properly but I did not know how to handle the situation. He stayed a while, looked at his daughter as he passed, then left and that was the way it was until Saturday.

He was not working Saturday, so he brought his cousin and a friend with him to see the baby. All the ladies had visitors at this time and he was not the centre of their attention, so he picked his daughter up and showed her as the proud father he was. He did this, as if he had being doing it every day.

On the visiting hour during the week, I did not have any visitors. One day the lady next to me said, "Put your hair up when the visitors come. You will look older." In the mornings when she woke up, she looked very old. She would take out her makeup, while I watched her with fascination, as she changed her appearance. Like a true artist painting the *Mona Lisa*, she worked her magic. Her husband looked a good deal younger than her. Maybe she was being kind to me asking me to put my hair up and look smart and a little more mature, when the visitors arrived. I am sure I did not carry makeup. It did not seem important then.

One morning during the week I was anxiously waiting for the nurses to bring my baby from the nursery. I immediately went to the bottom of the bed and there was an alien child, screaming his head off. His face was red and his hair was so fair. There were no eyebrows or lashes that I could see. I looked around at the mothers. Some had their babies and some were reading books. One was doing her nails, as her child was sleeping. I took the alien child and walked from bed to bed pushing him along the way, looking into each cot as I went. I got to the bed of the woman doing her nails. I saw my daughter in her cot at the bottom of her bed. I said to the mother. "This is your baby, you have mine." She moved down the bed and said, "Please keep him, he cries all the time, your baby is much prettier." I took my child and went.

On the day I was to leave the hospital, John came to collect me. A lovely West Indian nurse escorted us to the door. She said to John, "Ring for a taxi, we will wait here." John said, "We are fine, we will take the bus." She looked at him and said, "I will not be discharging this mother and baby until you get a taxi." He went without a word, rang for a taxi and we went home in style.

We arrived back to our room in St Mary's Road, Harlesden. John had painted the cot a lovely pink and when I dressed the cot with sheets I had made from pretty soft baby material and handsewn around the edges and her pretty pink and white blankets John bought, I was happy. I made lunch for John and he went back to work.

Chapter 26

St Mary's Road

One morning very early I was woken by the landlady, who was a West Indian lady. She came into my room. She was towering over me; all I could see was her wild hair and her eyes wide with anger looking at me. I'd had a bad night with my baby, she fed every two hours, on and off throughout the night. I had left the overhead light on and fallen asleep after the last feed. The light was over my head, with a cord dangling from it. The landlady turned it off with such force, banging the cord off the wall, all the while shouting abuse. "Do you know who is paying the electric bill?" she shouted. I was stunned and in shock, to be woken in this manner.

In the early days of emigration, a couple, after many sacrifices could save the money for the deposit on a house and purchase one. In order to be able to pay the mortgage they had to rent rooms. They did not want people living in their house; they needed the rent money to survive.

John started asking family and friends, if they'd heard of a room or flat for rent. He asked a work colleague. He was West Indian and his Mom had a house. The Mom said, "No, I don't want a white woman in my kitchen."

It was still West Indians who were more likely to rent to us. We walked in the evening looking at noticeboards in shop windows with the sign "Room to let "or sometimes, they would place a cardboard sign in a front room window. When I pushed the baby's pushchair up the path towards the house, where there was a room to let, when the owner saw us coming to the door, a woman waved frantically from her window saying "No."

I had no choice but to go to work when my baby was six weeks old. John could not get much sleep when he was on night work. My maternity leave finished at six weeks and John was keen that I went back to work. My sister knew what it was to live in one bedroom with a baby, as her baby was three weeks older than mine. She said I should look for an office job, the hours were shorter. I went to an agency. After an interview with a friendly lady she rang the company and spoke to their personnel manager. My name sounded foreign as it was of Indian descent. When she was giving information about me, she said, "I have a nice Irish lady here." She did not mention my name. I was now beginning to see how it was in the real world. When I went for the interview, I was asked where my surname had come from. I explained that I married a man with that name. Next question was "Where was he from? Where did you meet him?" It's a question that is still asked.

The wonder being, where were you, a nice Irish lady that you met him? Not mixing with your own kind. Ladbroke Grove was an area of emigrants. So you did not see racism in the raw.

I got the job as a filing clerk I would have done any job in the office that I was offered. I was a firm believer that if you did the same job day in, day out, you would become proficient at it, repetition and learning on the job makes you perform better every day. As it was my first job, I was employed as a filing clerk. This did not fit my theory as I had difficulty with spellings and it was a monotonous job with no opening for creativity. I was not as speedy as I would have wished. After a few months I sought a better job, both for my sanity and better pay.

The lady in the house looked after my baby. I was comforted by the fact that John would be in the same house and could see if anything was wrong. He worried me by saying that baby Louise cried. I did not want to leave her. When I went to the baby clinics, it was like a classroom. The nurse sat at the top of the room and the mothers sat facing her. There was a room full of mothers and their babies. The baby boom of the Sixties was in full flow. My turn came and I went up to the nurse. She weighed my baby then checked her out. She said she was doing very well. Then I told her I was going out to work and needed to dry up my milk, as I was breast feeding. She said you could get financial help to stay at home, if you couldn't afford it. It was not that John did not have money. We constantly tried to get a flat but to no avail. We would have to get a home of our own and that took a lot of money. We asked several people who had their own home. They said we would need £1,000 for a deposit to start with. That was a quarter to one fifth of the price of the house. We were emigrants so it was harder to get a mortgage... I was embarrassed as all the mothers were listening. I said very bravely, "I like going to work." She said no more and gave me the prescription for the tablets to dry up the breast milk.

Because we did not have a wedding reception John decided to have a splendid christening for Louise. He was preparing for weeks before. A friend worked on the American base and he paid him to get one or two bottles of spirits duty free. These he got over the next few weeks leading up to the christening.

The day came and my daughter was christened. I had knitted the white shawl and layette. She had a beautiful white lacy dress. The christening went very well. John told the landlady, of Louise's upcoming christening and that he would invite a few people and she agreed. So he invited family and one or two friends to our room.

It seemed like a lot of people but they fitted in while some stood chatting in the hall. They chatted away in little groups, cricket being high on the list of topics. I cooked and there was curry, rice with salads for all. Drinks flowed without incident.

There was a call for a family member to make a speech and give a toast. He was noted for his grand speeches. He quoted Shakespeare with great authority, ending with the cutting of the cake and a toast to the baby's good life, health and happiness. He then requested a plate and putting the first note down with a great flourish, the rest of the guests followed his example. The plate was soon filled with notes and I was presented with it.

I did not know this custom, but I was very glad of it. John and I went shopping for the baby the following week and bought her a pushchair.

Chapter 27

Moving Home Again

A cousin of John's told us about a room in a house on Minet Avenue which was let out in rooms. Every room had a tenant. The house was a hive of activity you inserted a shilling into the gas meter to cook, bathe and wash clothes. When I came home from work to cook and wash the baby's clothes and nappies, there was never any gas left. As the shilling dropped into the coin box, ladies would emerge from their rooms, start running hot water for baths, wash clothes and before my dinner was cooked the gas had run out again. Our heating system was a paraffin fire, sometimes I would rest a kettle on it to boil. I even cooked a pot of rice on it once when my shilling was finished and I was not willing to put another one into the meter. I would have to stay with the paraffin fire until I had finished the rice; it was a dangerous way of cooking.

When I finished feeding the baby I give her a bath and she settled down for the night. When I finished my bath, I would put the clothes in the water to soak and wash them, then dry the baby's nappies in front of the paraffin heater and fall exhausted into bed. On Thursday night I did not wash. I rinsed the nappies, soaked them and went to the laundrette on Saturday morning.

Louise was growing fast now. She was sitting up. I was feeding her on jars of dinner and dessert because she had advanced to grown-up food. One day I was eating an orange; she put her hand out through the bars of the cot for some. I gave her a little, I was very upset, that she had to put her hand out and ask for some. Why did I not know to offer her some? She was growing so fast it was an awakening; she had to move up to more solid foods. Around the same time she was sitting near where I left a cucumber on the table. I did not think she would eat one. I was making a salad. She had three little teeth.

I went into the kitchen, came back, saw little marks on the cucumber. I thought it was a mouse. I cut off the portion and threw it in the bin. I washed the rest of the cucumber. I came back again and saw her this time with the cucumber in her hand, biting into it with her little teeth. It is a learning process for all mothers. Every action by their first baby is amazing. I had a lot of knowledge to draw from helping my mother with my young siblings, but to experience it with my first child was wonderful.

We moved to another house on Minet Avenue just two doors up and we were glad to move to a less occupied house. The room was clean and there was the use of a dining room which we did not take up. As it was not part of the rent we would have to pay more. There were only two people using the kitchen, the landlord and I. I was happy; I washed the floors and polished them every weekend. The landlord was from the island of St Vincent in the Caribbean. His daughter and her husband had the house next door. One day, John's cousin who worked with the landlord told his family, "The landlord is talking about Marie, John's wife; he said, he is renting to a white woman and she kept the place nasty." John's cousin knew that was not true but he repeated it to John's family and it got back to me. Saying he had bad tenants gave the landlord status. He had property and he rented. If I brought a meal from the kitchen to our room and left crumbs on the table, before I could put the plate down he would knock on our door and tell me about it. I was the topic of conversation among John's family as gossip travelled fast.

The landlord and his son-in-law were in the kitchen when I entered. I said, "My husband's family are all talking about me. You said a white woman, renting from you is nasty and does not keep the place clean. What you said was not true." His son-in-law went mad at him, pulling out drawers and saying to him, 'look at the state you keep your cupboards in. You are so nasty you need to clean them before you die of food poisoning.' He stood there like a little boy shame-faced. I was happy with the result.

After some months passed, I went to pay my rent to the landlord. He was standing at his front door talking to his friend. He said, "I need your room." He would not take the rent money and said, "My family are arriving from St Vincent in the morning

"I need the room, you have to go." I felt he had his friend with him for support, as he had put off telling us until the last moment. His wife, daughter, her husband and his son, all adults were arriving the following morning, he needed our room to accommodate some of them. I went back to my room, sat on the bed and told John what had happened. He went to speak to the landlord. John said to him, "We have nowhere to go." He told John that he had got a room for us at the bottom of Minet Avenue and would help us move.

I was devastated. John was working that night. It was about 5pm. We went to see the room; it was between the size of a small room and a medium room. John set up the cot.

There was the bed, the cot, a wardrobe and that was all. I put our clothes in the wardrobe and packed as much as I could under the bed. We did not have a lot as John always said, "Do not buy extras as we may have to move, we do not want the trouble of moving a lot of stuff. We will keep looking for a room. This room will have to do for now, if the people do not want you in their house you have to go." We had to eat sitting on the bed, with the suitcase between us as a table. John went off to work.

There was a knock on the door. A box of groceries had been delivered from a local Jamaican shop. The house was occupied by Jamaicans. I said I did not order the groceries. There was food in the box that would not generally have been included in my groceries. The landlord who brought the box to my room said that maybe my husband had ordered them on his way to work. He said I had to pay the man at the door for the groceries. I paid for the groceries as I did not want to get drawn into a quarrel. It could have been ordered by someone else in the house. I did not want to make a fuss. I was on my own with my daughter and was feeling very uneasy. John had not ordered the food. I used what I could of the food.

The next day we went to talk to our old landlord's son-in-law. He and his wife were reasonable people. He was very understanding. He realised his father-in-law had not given us proper notice and so he moved his family around. He did the room up and in a week's time we moved in to the son-in-law's house. I was more settled there as I knew the landlord and his wife. I was very scared living in the house at the bottom of Minet Avenue. I did not know anyone.

The son-in-law had a great love for music and could be seen and heard playing Lovers rock on a Saturday morning and any opportunity he got. He knew all the songs and would conduct the music like he was conducting an orchestra. If he had musical training, I am sure he would have been very successful. He had a real passion for it. A few years later we went to a function and who should I see but the son-in-law conducting a small band. He was oblivious to everyone in the hall. I am sure members of the band thought him a strange fellow, as he was not part of their group. I knew he was the happiest man on earth. The hall was full and people were dancing. They paid him no heed.

Chapter 28

Going Home On Holiday

Five months after the birth of Louise, I was in need of a holiday and wanted to go home to Ireland. When you have emigrated to another country you start to lose your identity. It starts with a little adjustment to your new environment. People correct your way of speaking and little things like if I called a swede a turnip, my local vegetable shop would correct me. I would point to a swede. If I asked for a turnip I would be give a white baby turnip.

You feel lost, you stop looking in crowds to see if you recognise people from your home town. Once a neighbour from home said to me, "I saw you on Wembley high street. I knocked on the bus window, but you did not see me."

When you return from your holiday, you feel rejuvenated. You know who you are, because people on your road, know your family. They know your family background. They know you come from good stock. Living in another country you have to build your history slowly over many years. In a foreign country you are the beginning of a tribe with no ancestors of good repute. Life starts with you. So I wrote to Mammy and said I was coming home for a holiday.

She was there to greet me at the station. She immediately took to Louise and we got the bus home. As we walked down our road, unmarried twins I knew, who lived on our road and were older than me, approached to greet us. Mammy whispered to me, "I did not tell anyone that you got married." That said she would not have mentioned the baby. I now had to contend with being an unmarried mother on our street. Mammy would have thought, it was not their business. I was thankful she had told my aunts.

When we got indoors, Louise was taken to my family's hearts; she was held, cosseted and played with. I was not used to all the attention they gave her, as I did not have any close family in England to visit; my sister was struggling with her own life.

It was time for Louise's nap so I put her into my bed to sleep and the house was quiet. The two younger sisters had gone to school. I heard Louise laughing. I thought how can she be laughing on her own. I could see the bedroom door, no one entered her room. I opened the door and there was my brother playing with her on the bed. Our house is a cottage and he climbed through the window. I chased him out and he left laughing. I was strict; she had to have her rest.

My Dad loved to hold her and started feeding her a little of his dinner. I said, "Daddy, she's too young for grown-up food." He used to say, "Do you think she looks like me?" My Mammy said "Yes" to him. I did not think she looked anything like him. She was very pretty and petite.

My friend Sorcha came to see me and we planned an outing. We went to town and got a taxi. Sorcha told the taxi driver I was married to an Indian prince. She's a lovely friend who I am still in touch with. She is a hopeless romantic. John would laugh if he knew. I am sure at the time my parents would view John differently if he was a prince. We travelled to Lough Dreg to the village of Killaloe on the river Shannon. Its scenery is second to none, it was a hot summer's day, the Taxi radio played the Top of the Pops, on a Sunday afternoon.

The Loch is one of three on the river Shannon which is the longest river in Europe. It starts in Shannon Pot in Cavan. There are three large lochs, Loch Allen is mostly in county Leitrim; Loch Ree means lake of the kings. It starts from Roscommon to Athlone, County Westmeath. Loch Dreg is the largest loch on the river Shannon.

We sat and had tea in the lakeside hotel overlooking the lake and the rolling hills. We chatted as if distance and new experiences gained did not exist, at ease in our company. I was happy with our conversation, me catching up with current events in Limerick, who is doing what these days. Then we wandered around Killaloe, taking in part of the scenery, on our way back to the taxi. The taxi driver had agreed to wait for us as it was a nice day. We said we would get another taxi back so as not to trouble him, He said he would get a light lunch and enjoyed the sights and waited for us.

At home I would put Louise in her pushchair in the front garden. Mammy would take her and the pushchair inside the house. I would put her out again. It was at that time I saw a girl from my class at school dressed in her school uniform. She passed in front of our house, on her way home from school for her dinner. Now I knew why Mammy brought my daughter inside; she did not want me to be the talk of the school. I said to Mammy, "Why is she still at school?" only to be told, "Marie, you would be doing your leaving certificate this year if you stayed at home and went to school." I didn't reply. That girl later became a famous Irish artist.

I had been away, growing up, getting married and having a baby. Home and school was so far from my mind. It seemed to me that time had stood still at home. So much had happened to me, I thought years had passed. It was only three years; she was in her final months at school. It was a shock to my system to see her in her school uniform. At home, time and lives moved in a measured uniform way where I had jumped on to a moving ramp and shot into the future like a firework.

I had to pay a visit to all my aunts and show my daughter off. My various aunts treated me very well always a welcome, a high tea and questions about England.

The high point of my visit was when I went to see my granny and my aunt at their home. I took a walk with Louise over to the island. I lingered over the bridge to take in one of the most beautiful sights, a view of King John's Castle. I always loved my granny and my aunt. As I walked, I remembered going to granny's on Sunday night. Mammy would say, "I will take you with me to the island." We would take to the middle of our road, my hand linked in her arm, past the O' Donoghues, the shop, the O' Reillys, the O'Brians, the Meaneys and down to Lanny Fraser's rounding the corner to the sight of King John's Castle on the river Shannon.

We strolled or brusquely walked, depending on the weather. We came into view of St Munchin's Church, old as the hills, and the Treaty Stone, viewed by many visiting tourists.

We stepped on the bridge, the river Shannon rushing, swirling waters of blue and grey, dancing in white surf between the grey stones. The elegant façade of the castle fitted snugly into the landscape. The hills in the distance were surrounded in gold, as the sun went down. The excitement built as we turned by the watch tower, down the side of the river, beside the old grave yard, hidden behind high mossy walls. It was out of use now for many a year. We passed the ancient swimming area, where young boys laughed, splashed and swam many years ago. We came to a little passageway, with a raised path near the men's weightlifting club. I was the first to see granny and my aunt at the upstairs window, looking out for us; I read my aunt's lips saying, "Mammy there is Mary." The sun reflected off the house, windows were mirrored eyes, set in a redbrick house of gold.

Chapter 29

Granddad

Sadness came to our cottage as it visited all the homes in Farranshone at one time or another. On a nice sunny day it was our custom to sit at the front of our house and after Mammy had scrubbed us and washed our hair, it would gleam in the sunlight. She always said that your health shows in your hair, if it was shiny, you were in good health. I saw Granny's neighbour approaching our house; this was very unusual as I had never seen her there before. When she got nearer she looked unhappy and serious and called out "Is your Mammy there?" I ran into the house and called Mammy. As she saw Granny's neighbour she knew that all was not well. The lady said, "I am so sorry Mary. It is your Daddy." Mammy started to cry, we all looked on in amazement not quite understanding. I knew it was very serious. I gathered it was about my grandfather. Something had happened to him.

I recalled the last time I had seen him. He came to our house delivering a cake. My Granny was a great cook. She baked wonderful cakes and pies and would also buy suet from the butcher's and melt it down in the oven and pour it into a small white enamel bowl with a blue rim. She would give it to Mammy to roast or fry with. Mammy had asked my Granddad to stay a while and look after us while she ran quickly into town to do some shopping. I can remember him standing in the dining room with his back to the door that led to the hall and out the front door. His head was inclined in the direction of the window looking down the road to see if Mammy was coming back. I was anxiously awaiting the return of Mammy, as one of my younger siblings was sitting in a pool of water crying. I assume he had wet himself. Granddad looked very uncomfortable; all of a sudden Mammy arrived at the gate and rushed in apologising. I knew all was well and Granddad left with a great sense of relief.

My Mammy went to my granny's every Sunday night after the children were in bed; she sometimes took me or my sister. My grandfather was a man of habit, a serious man he would wind up the clock on the mantelpiece at the same time every night. When Mammy visited she took this as a signal to leave. When Granny mentioned this to grandfather he was very upset, he was only doing what he had done since he was married. He would not have made his daughter feel uncomfortable for the world.

Mammy later told me that granddad was on his bicycle delivering a cake that granny had made for her sister Kate. He collapsed and passed instantly. It is funny what people say when you are gone. The doctor at the hospital said granddad had all his teeth; they were in perfect condition. Mammy said that he brushed them every day with a mixture of ash from the fire and salt. I was four when my grandfather died in 1949, aged 64. Grandfather was the assistant postmaster of the General Post Office in Limerick. He started as a postman and worked his way up. He was a decent, hard-working man and the love of my Granny's life. She would take out her hanky and cry on Sunday night when she talked about him and say things would be different if he were alive.

Chapter 30

Granny Stories

O n My Sunday visits to Grannies after our supper we would settle by the fire and my Granny would relate stories about when she was a young girl. As with all children my Mammy would sometimes catch my aunt's eye. They had heard it all before. Mammy would look at my aunt with raised eyebrows. They would still settle down to listen. I loved these stories and I am sorry that I did not ask more questions. When I was young, children were seen and not heard. My Granny would go back to her childhood and tell us about her Mammy who was born in 1856 and died in 1912. The famine in Ireland was from 1845 for seven years until 1852. Ireland was still very poor fifty years later. My Granny had a sister who died of water on the brain and the nuns would come from the convent to visit her. As my Granny was the eldest, it was her responsibility to help nurse her sister. On the day of her sister's funeral the neighbours took my great grandmother whose name was Catherine to their house to console and comfort her. It was late and my Granny was making her way up the steps to the loft, where her room was. Her father told her "come and sit by the fire awhile". He made her a cup of tea and gave her a slice of bread, butter and jam. She never forgot it, as in their house they were never given butter and jam together. Times were very hard. Love and gratitude were shown in little actions. People did not always wear their hearts on their sleeve.

One day my great grandmother was at Mass when she was told by neighbours that her name was on the noticeboard. A solicitor wanted to get in touch with her. That was the way additional information was communicated, if someone was trying to trace you. A solicitor wanted her to get in touch with him with regards to a bequest from a deceased uncle, who lived in America. There was great excitement with neighbours wishing them well. Early in the day Grannie's sister Kate was sent on messages and there was a farthing change. She bought a bag of sherbet as she thought her Mammy would forget with all the excitement. She was just going up the steps to the bedroom and her Mammy remembered. Aunt Kate was in big trouble. Her Mammy said "A bird in the hand is worth two in the bush. Talk of a bequest was not having it in your hand".

With the bequest their fortune changed a little and it was decided that Granny who was eighteen in 1902, should go to America and work there as they were in contact with their relatives. Granny was fitted out from head to toe at Todd's, our equivalent to Harrods in England. After a tearful goodbye at the train station in Limerick, she travelled to Queenstown in Cork by train and boarded the SS *Campania* on the 11th May, 1902. It was a ship on the Cunard line and she arrived in New York on the 17th May, 1902. At that time a lot of people did not return to Ireland for many years. So leaving Ireland for America was comparable to a funeral. The older generation would have passed away, they would say this is the last time you will see me alive, I will be gone when you return. From 1848 to 1950 6,000,000 people emigrated from Queenstown, County Cork to countries all over the world where they would work, make a life for themselves and contribute to their family back home.

When she arrived at New York harbour she had to go through clearing at Ellis Island which was a harrowing experience. It was a massive hall with wooden floor and rows upon rows of brown benches. How long she waited I can only imagine. Some people would not be allowed to disembark if they did not pass the medical and would be hospitalised, quarantined or returned to their country of origin. She passed her medical and was asked how much money she had. She showed the customs officer five pounds. They translated it into 20 dollars, it cost the same for her fare to America, he was happy that she had sufficient funds She carried on her journey to Philadelphia by train. On arriving she was taken to St John's RC Church where after she rested and was refreshed she was given directions to her aunt's.

She was walking down a road that her aunt lived in. It had very large houses. In one of the gardens there were boys playing baseball. One of the boys saw her and called out, 'There is cousin Delia from Ireland.' They came and helped her with her bag; she was made very welcome by all. They were a very wealthy family and did not want her to work because they owned department stores. The weather was very hot. They bought her a new wardrobe of more suitable clothes for the climate and catered for all her needs.

They took the clothes she arrived from Ireland in and when visitors came they would be brought out and shown. All admired the craftsmanship of the Irish Tweed suit, the finish of the work and the fine Irish linen slips and undergarments, the lace bodice and her kid boots beautifully made. These discussions were taken very seriously and there was great pride in what Ireland was able to produce and the quality of its workmanship.

Chapter 31

Granny Found Work

My Granny told her aunt that she came to work and help her family and they understood. She was introduced to her auntie's friend who hired her as a lady's companion. Granny learned to bake beautiful Christmas cakes with almonds sitting on top, peaches and pear pies. The house had a butler, a large kitchen, a chef and kitchen staff. When the chef was baking the special Christmas cakes and pies the lady of the house and Granny would make them with him from family recipes. She spent nine years in America. Her way of life was influenced during her time there.

Until the end of her days she had three meals a day and did not eat in between. She had breakfast at 9am, lunch at 12.30pm and supper at 6pm. You could set your clock by it. On my visits to Granny's she would serve supper to my aunt and mother who were identical twins. The supper comprised of cold lamb with salad and a slice of her peach or pear pie. I cannot remember her offering a second slice of pie, or them asking for more. They were used to her ways and she would have thought one slice was sufficient. When the table was cleared and washed up, a place was laid for me and I had the same as my aunt and Mammy. I heard her mention once that children had their meals in the nursery and came to say goodnight to their parents after their supper.

My Granny's mother was taken ill and her father wrote to her and asked her to come home to Ireland. He thought she was away long enough and was not married and he needed her help with the family. My great grandmother had a dream that a postman had given her a letter and when she went into the shop the next day the postman came in. His name was John. He was well respected in the area. He said to my great grandmother, "I hear that your daughter is coming home from America. How is she?" They had known one another at school, after some talk an understanding was arrived at by the shopkeeper and Great Grandmother and my grandfather. Before Granny could come home from America my great grandmother died.

My Granny received the news of her Mammie's death before she left America. The butler came to her with the letter on a silver tray; a black border surrounded the envelope as was the custom with letters announcing death. She knew it was bad news. Her Mammy had said before she died that if John and Delia got together and agreed, the wedding plans were to go ahead even though my Granny would be in mourning. My Granny, Delia Gleeson was married to John Barry on the 3rd June 1914 at St John's Cathedral in Limerick City. She and my grandfather were very happy until my granddad died. It was a good marriage. He died years before her. Tears would come to her eyes when she talked about him.

On a Sunday night Granny would sometimes talk about her son Christy. It was very painful for her as he passed away from tuberculosis. He was a very handsome young man, a junior reporter for the *Limerick Leader*. He was keen on sports and played football, did weight training and had a steady girlfriend. One day after sports he told my Granny that he was not feeling very well. She told him to go out in the back yard where the toilet was if he was going to be sick. When he came back indoors he said that he had brought up blood. She was very worried and said that she would take him to the doctor's surgery. He insisted on going alone. He had another haemorrhage in the doctor's surgery and he was diagnosed with tuberculosis. It was decided the best treatment for him was in a nursing home in the mountains as the air would be better for his recovery.

My Mammy said that when he played football he left his clothes on the grass and they got damp. He would then wear the damp clothes. There were no changing facilities in those days. Mammy would air all our clothes on an iron pulley after washing and drying them Mammy would also line us up after breakfast for a spoon of cod liver oil and an iron supplement called Parish's food. It was not our favourite time, there were strong protests from my siblings. I understood she did her best to keep us healthy in the cold and rain of the Irish winter. There was always the fear of losing a child to TB. There was no point in saying no you did not want any, she was a very strong-willed woman and I did not think it was worth arguing the point.

Granddad and Granny had to hire a pony and trap to visit their son. It was very far from Limerick and they could not go as often as they wished. On one such visit Christy asked them, could he come home to die, so they brought him home. He was lovingly nursed by his parents and sisters. One day while his sisters were looking out the window of his room at the river Shannon, Granny sat by his side holding his hand. My Mammy said that the daffodils would soon be in bloom along the banks of the Shannon. He said he would be gone before then. They kept looking out the window as they did not want him to see the tears flow down their cheeks.

Tuberculosis was very prevalent in Ireland at that time. There was a stigma attached to the disease. Parents were not happy for their children to mix or marry into a family that was affected by TB, in case they got the disease. On the morning that Christy died my grandfather went to Mass. On his return as he came up the road to his house, all the neighbours came out of their homes to greet him and to offer their condolences. That was how he heard the news that his son had passed away.

Chapter 32

It Is Never Too Late To Have A Happy Childhood

Remember the good times and not dwell on the hard times, is the way to revisit your childhood. On my Sunday visit to my Granny's with Mammy on a fine summer's evening I would play outside Granny's house, with a girl I became friends with. She lived on the road and I heard Granny say there were twenty-one children in the family. Her Mammy was a small woman and I wondered how that would be possible. Where did they fit in the house? Some were grown up and left home before the younger ones were born. One girl was a nun with the Poor Clares, a very strict religious order, one boy was a boxer and one I remember had scarring on his face. I asked Granny how he got his scars and she said, his Mammy had been making soap on the stove and he'd pulled it down on himself. I was curious. "Why did she make soap?" She told me it was cheaper than buying it. She had a large family and a lot of washing to do.

Granny's house was on a street of red-bricked houses with a sitting room off the hall, the stairs leading off the living room went to two bedrooms. The bathroom or wash-house, if you prefer to call it, was in a small yard in an outhouse. It had a wooden raised platform with an enamel basin and enamel water jug, towel and carbolic soap on a soap plate. If I smell carbolic soap today it brings to mind the scent of Granny's bathroom. The toilet was in a separate outhouse, all spotlessly clean.

One day I was invited to my friend's house. As we all gathered around the fire, her Daddy took a large bar of chocolate from his pocket. There was absolute silence as all eyes were transfixed on him, he broke it into squares and gave us all one square each, with two to his wife and two for himself. It was like sharing the wafer at Mass. We all silently sucked on our piece of chocolate with relish, making it last as long as humanly possible.

While it melted down the back of our throats. I can still remember that chocolate if I close my eyes and the kind generosity of her Daddy, who had little and shared all. I knew you did not have to be rich to enjoy the simple pleasures of life.

My friend and I had a favourite pastime; it was to have a tea party with our imaginary dolls. Broken bits of china were cups and saucers. The disused British army graveyard was a few doors up from Granny's. The graveyard was in use up to the end of the occupation pre-1916. We would enter by the caretaker's front garden. There was a large gate to the side that led to the graveyard. It was used for a hearse to pass through.

There were some very large white marble gravestones. We would sit on them and play. I am sure the departed were very happy with our company. We had no fear as we regarded this place as our playground.

The caretaker was an old woman, Mrs Condell. She wore very dark clothes, very Victorian in look and sat on a rocking chair in the front garden. When the sun shone the garden seemed very large to me.

I revisited it recently and found that the garden was not as large or as long as I had thought. When you are small everything seems much larger in relation to your size. We would sit with her for a while, asking her, "Mrs Condell, have you seen any ghosts?" She would take a little box from her pocket, take a pinch of snuff and sneeze into a very brown handkerchief.

She would tell the story. She had all of our attention as she spoke. "One night, while I was looking out from an upstairs window on to the graveyard, I saw an elderly woman, dressed in a long dress, standing by one of the graves. I expect the lady came to say goodbye to her son, before she left this world." We wanted to hear more but that was it.

Sometimes my Granny would give me a jug to go to the dairy across the road; she knew what time the milking was done and when the milk was delivered in urns to the shop. It was a shop on the outside but on the inside it looked more like a dairy, with large urns of milk and ladles the size of pint, half pint and quart. I would ask for a pint of milk and the lady would take it out of the urn with a pint measure, a shiny silver ladle, and pour the milk warm and still frothy, into my cream jug with a blue band around the edge, while I looked on with interest. We had our milk delivered in bottles, this was a novelty.

Granny told us about one of the mothers on the street who sat up knitting a pair of socks all night so that her child could wear them to school in the morning.

On a hot summer's day, Granny asked me to go to the shops on the estate. (The estate was built after my Granny's red-bricked house). I would get a threepenny bag of dulse and a six penny cup of periwinkles. They were delicious.

Granny said the dulse was high in iron and sea minerals, magnesium and calcium. I have tried them recently while on holiday in Kilkee in County Clare. They do not have the same hold on me. My taste buds have changed.

My Mammy would say it is getting late; we will make our way home before closing time. Mammy would rather not pass the pub when the men were coming out. I asked her if she was afraid when she was on her own. Mammy said, "If you are out after dark always walk briskly, as if you have somewhere to go and no one will bother you."

We would walk up Granny's road with my Granny and aunt waving us off. We would walk through a passageway with a high wall by the side of a disused graveyard on out to the side of the river Shannon. On one such night I heard a voice saying, 'One day, no one you know will be living in that house.' Strangers live in my Granny's house now. I did not say anything to Mammy.

On a clear night you could see millions of stars in the navy blue sky and shooting stars falling through the night sky. The river was blue-black flowing past at high tide. We would see King John's Castle in the moonlight and over the Thomond Bridge we would go. If we passed someone they would say "Good night Mam," to Mammy and she would reply, "It is a lovely night, thank God." We made our way up the familiar Farranshone and home to bed.

Chapter 33

First Real Home

I shopped in the corner shop on Minet Avenue and would always ask the shopkeeper, who was a very nice Welsh lady, if she knew of any flats for rent. One day she said that a Spanish lady who lived on Harley Road had a flat to rent. I brought my little girl with me and we made our way to her house. Louise was now two and very petite with long curly hair with fair highlights when the sun shone on her hair, I always had her dressed nicely. She was like my little doll. The landlady would be very taken by her. I would talk to her as I went shopping or to the laundrette. I would say, 'When you are sixteen do not ask me can you leave school. The answer will be no. Friends will leave for work, you will stay on at school.' There was no comment from her. She was very young. Years later she told me when friends left school after GCSEs, 'I told my friends that there was no point asking Mom could I leave school. The answer would be no.'

We knocked on Mrs Fernandez's door and I said to her, "The lady in the shop said you had a flat to rent." She said, "I cannot rent to couples with children as I have a dog. He may attack them." She then asked me, "Would you like to see the flat?" I began to feel a little hopeful. No one had ever asked me to look around a flat that they were not going to rent to me. She showed me the flat. The dog, an Alsatian, calmly followed us around as we went through the flat, a sitting room, a bedroom, bathroom, separate toilet and large kitchen. It was my heart's desire. Again I asked, "Would you change your mind about renting us the flat? We live very quietly. My husband works nights and there would only be me and my little girl in the flat." She said, "No. If it was not for my dog, I would rent the flat to you. He might attack your daughter." I tried to convince her. "I will be very careful coming up the stairs." She was adamant.

The next day I went to the shop for milk. The shopkeeper told me that Mrs Fernandez's dog had died during the night. I did not waste any time. I took my daughter with me and we knocked on her door. It was answered by Mrs Fernandez. I said, "I am so sorry for your loss." She invited me into her living room. Her husband was sitting at the table. She said to me, "If we had not had a cage at the back of the door to catch any post dropped from the letter box, so that our dog would not eat it, we would say you poisoned our dog." We walked to the hall door. She showed me the letterbox. I let her talk. Then I said to her in front of her husband, "You said you would let me have the flat, if it were not for the dog." There was not much she could say, there was no way out for her. I got the flat and moved in later that day; it was the flat of my dreams. I have always been grateful to the dog. He was old, he was a soul mate and somehow, he felt my grief.

Mrs Fernandez got another Alsatian. If she was in the hall downstairs when we made our way up the stairs, she would hold the dog by the collar and push him forward in a threatening way. She would say 'Que malo, que malo" "as if to attack us. The Alsatian never did attack us. She made it look like she was making a joke, she knew and I knew she meant it. She had no family herself and it was her way of protecting the downstairs against intruders, my daughter and I. I did not care once this ritual was completed and I got to the top of the stairs, backs to the wall and reached my flat.

John had been working shift work two weeks nights and two weeks days, six days then six nights a week from April 1961 to 1966. In the summer months when he tried to sleep it was impossible. The noise of children's laughter when playing on the street after school, or all day in the school holidays, would wake him up. After his dinner when he went out in the cold air he would be sick. He could not hold down his food. I told him to hand in his notice.

I asked the personnel manager where I worked if they had any vacancies. They were training men in plastics, in a factory in Colindale and the manager arranged for John to take part. John enjoyed the work and felt he did well. He mentioned that the other men training would do a little work and walk about talking to other factory workers while he worked. The company would offer work to some of the men at the end of the course. Two of them were not employed. John and another West Indian man, all the white men were employed. I went back to the personnel department and talked to the manager.

I told him what had happened. He looked into it and offered John a job on his maintenance team. No words were said about the fairness or unfairness of the decision not to employ John in the factory in Colindale. He was just happy he got a job. He worked there for twenty-seven years as a foreman and was made redundant when they closed down Unigate due to milk not being delivered directly to homes. Housewives were now purchasing milk at the supermarkets with their groceries. It was no longer necessary to have milk delivered. It was a sign of changing times. The maintenance work John did was on the milk floats giving them a renewed life, doing plastic repair and painting them with his team. They visited all the Unigate branches in the London area.

After two years of unemployment, John got a job in the hospital as a porter. He felt the wages were very low. I told him not to do overtime but he would still do it, which enabled him to bring home a respectable wage. His light-hearted banter with a patient when wheeling them to theatre lightened their load. I met a young man who John got a job for. He was a slow learner. It was just like John to speak up for someone, who could not do so for himself. John was a likeable person, people gravitated towards him, he was quick to make friends. Friends respected him for his no-nonsense attitude; he knew when to talk and when to be silent.

At the end of a cricket season a party was always held. He gave the presentation speech and presented the prizes. He did this as if he had been doing it every day of his life. I was amazed as I would have been embarrassed to stand there and give a speech. He was a people's person. On one occasion, at a party John was sitting in the middle of a group of men holding court on cricket. They would say 'John, what do you think of the poor performance of the West Indian cricket team? What are they going to do now, having not performed well once again?' He gave his opinion. Cricket is the subject that levels all classes who hold a love for the game.

After he passed on, our family was invited to a wedding of a young man we knew. He spoke highly of John; he told us that he had no money when he came to attend school in England. John used to give him pocket money when he saw him and later he told him, 'When you get a job, never take more than one item on credit and when you have paid it off, you can get something else.' He found this to be very good advice. A little advice given and forgotten is always surprising, when one finds that it is taken up and acted upon.

John would have been happy to know that he had an influence on a young man's life. Sometimes a member of the younger generation could be seen chatting with him in the back garden. If they told him something he did not judge. If asked for advice, he would give it. He saw no shadows in his life. It was right or wrong, black or white.

His cousins' sons said to me after his death, "We do not see anyone to replace uncle, as the head of the family. He was the one you could turn to." They could always guarantee a private conversation that went no further.

Chapter 34

Cricket

John and his cousins always played cricket. They played in the Caribbean and they played from the moment they set foot on English soil. They had formed their own cricket team, single men against married men, If they were short a man, then and only then would they invite another to join the family team, just to make up the numbers. The cricketer would have to have a reputation for being a superior bowler, or very good at batting. When the elders of the family came to the UK they studied the cricket leagues, signed up and played different teams every week. When the family was settled the elders returned home.

Going to a cricket match all day meant preparing a picnic for the children and myself. Packing nappies for baby, change of clothes if necessary, bottles of milk and anything else required. I did not go to all the matches. I got my chores done, when it was a home match, I could join them later. I enjoyed it, if the away match was at the seaside, which they arranged once a year, they would hire a coach and make an event of the day. The men went on the cricket pitch and the woman promenaded beside the sea front. They stopped at the shops to buy sticks of rock that were never eaten, buy souvenirs made in China, ate fish and chips at a cafe and had an enjoyable day.

I also liked it, if the match was in a nice residential area. I would wander in and out the roads looking at expensive houses and beautiful gardens.

Children would eat from the mothers of whatever family they were playing with and I would feed who was around me at the time. The men had tea in the pavilion, for which they paid a small fee.

John got new cricket regalia. I thought that the white cricket jumper was expensive so I decided to knit it myself. It would work out cheaper. I can knit and can follow a pattern. The problem is I have never got the tension right. I am a loose knitter. When I knitted children's layettes I would knit the smallest size and it would fit the baby up to a year old.

I started my husband's jumper making sure it had a thin line of green, yellow and green bands around the sleeves and bottom of the jumper and I was very happy with the result. After pressing it with a damp cloth and laying it out on the table, it was perfect in every way. On the day of a big match it was finished and I presented it to John. He put it on and was completely swallowed up in it. He was very nice about it. He said to "Give it to your dad".

On my next visit home I gave it to my dad who liked a Guinness or two and had thickened around his waist. He was a keen gardener and had a beautiful garden, so I suggested that he wore it while he did his work. To my surprise my Daddy who had a great sense of humour, laughingly said, "Would you mind if I wore it to the pub. My friend's wife always knits him his jumpers and he wears them with a great sense of pride. He is wearing a canary yellow one at the moment, so can I say Mammy knit it for me. That will make him sit up." I said I would be delighted.

One of John's cousins named Elmo was a tall, good looking man with a voice that carried. No one would deny that he liked a good bottle of wine as well. At a Sunday cricket match fitted out in his whites and looking every bit the professional cricketer, he took up his position waiting for the call to bat. We were at an away game in the leafy outskirts of London, a very English suburb. As his cousins played, Elmo coached them in a loud voice, from the sidelines. If they dropped a catch or did not get one, he let rip, to the amusement of the wives of the opposition and to the embarrassment of the wives of the family. He had a word of advice for every cricketer as they walked from the wicket. When they were bowled out, he let them know where their failings lay. Elmo was the last man called.

The wives of the opposition sat upright to see the coach as he proudly took to the field, to win for his team. Not so, he was called last for a good reason. He was out for a duck. They could not help laughing as Elmo came off the field with his head held high to applause.

He had provided an afternoon's entertainment, even if the family team did not think so. In the pavilion bar that evening, there was much good hearted discussion on his antics, while hardliners dissected the game. They went through every bat and bowl, with many a pat on the back and a smile for the cricketer who did well. If he spoke they would listen, as he was the man with the knowledge today. There was always the player who thought that he was unfairly bowled out as the ball never touched his inside leg.

The men lingered while I anxiously wanted to go home to get the children settled for the night and prepare supper. When they got older the children had to iron school uniforms. I had to give them their school dinner money and they would now say, I rarely had the correct change. Then we all headed to bed, to wake early for work and school in the morning.

At the end of the season there was a big party and presentations made for the highest scores for the season, Man of the matches etc . . .

The wives cooked dhal puri, fried fish, fried chicken, curried mutton, rice, salads and coleslaw, cake and dessert. The drink flowed and a good time was had by all.

Chapter 35

Work Tea Break

In the early years when I arrived in the UK, I only had contact with its citizens when I worked. Family and friends were Trinidadian, Guyanese and Grenadian. I did not make friends outside John's family and his friends. I went to work every day did my work and came home. Doing agency work, did not allow me to get to know work colleagues and I had a lot to do at home.

I kept my head down and got on with my work, had half an hour for lunch and finished at four thirty to allow me to pick up my child from the nanny.

When I worked at one company, the accounts department would go to morning break together. On more than one occasion the talk would be on emigrants and their bad points. One lady was saying how a black man was a thief on her road. When this type of talk came up, I felt very low. I felt I should be protective of whoever they were talking about, as if it was a slur on my family. There was no one in my husband's family who was in trouble with the law. I will go back to the time when I had a brush with the law.

On a hot summer's day during the school holidays, with nothing for us to do, we gathered in groups on the road, bored and looking for adventure. Apples were ripe and after some discussion, the bigger boys on our road went over the wall and into the orchard across the road from our house. The actor Richard Harris's mother and family lived there. They had an orchard with apples, gooseberries, red currants, a greenhouse with grapes and other fruits. The back entrance, across the road from the front gate to our cottage, was a wide wooden door set in a high wall, with a smaller door cut into it. One of the boys who went over the wall opened the small door. Suddenly there was a hive of activity as we swarmed like bees in through the small door. One of the boys kept watch on the house to let us know if the lady of the house would walk down the path to investigate, who had invaded her orchard.

I immediately got busy with the red currants putting them in to my pocket. It left a dark stain and destroyed my favourite red corduroy dungarees. I helped myself to some apples and tucked them into my blouse. The rest of the children were scurrying around helping themselves to fruit.

There was a young boy who would run in and out of the entrance keeping watch for the guard. When we were previously in the orchard, he called out, "The guard is coming, the guard is coming." A guard would be cycling up the road; we would all run out, pushing and falling out of the small door of the orchard, disappearing into every house, leaving the road silent and empty.

He called wolf once too often. This time when he called he was ignored. I thought he was shouting too long, so I looked up. "The guard is coming, the guard is coming." He appeared to be crying. Sure enough, the guard, a dark menacing shadow was standing behind the boy. Tears were running down the boy's face. I thought I must make myself scarce. I hid behind the greenhouse. The guard lined up all the children by the side of the path and took out his black notebook and wrote down their names and addresses. Then he said, "Is there anyone else here?" A voice said, 'Marie is behind the greenhouse.' The guard walked towards the greenhouse and me. When he made his way around the greenhouse, I went the other way. He went towards the back calling all the time, "Marie don't be frightened, don't be frightened." I had made my way to the front near the path. I took off like a bat out of hell, passed the line of children beside the path, a sea of faces with startled expressions, out the door I went, away down the road like the road runner to Meany's field panting and my heart racing.

Luckily for me, I still had the apples in my blouse, it was getting late, I could tell by where the sun was sitting in the sky, it was past my dinner time. I was starving and I was afraid to go home in case the guard was waiting for me. The apples tasted good and eventually I made my way home, when all was quiet. As I came in the door I could see Daddy sitting in his chair. Dinner was finished, the table was cleared. Daddy said, "Marie, the guard was knocking at this front door, for you." I must have looked shocked. He smiled and said, "Next time don't get caught." I breathed a sigh of relief and sat down at the table. Mammy served me a hot dinner; she had saved my dinner for me, I did not look up from my plate. I did not dare utter a word as I was not sure how it would go for me. We were scared of going into the orchard for some time. I thought it advisable to let the boys get the apples and plead with my brother for one, which was no easy task, as they were as precious as gold.

John's family were all hard working. They kept to themselves, played cricket in the summer and cards in the winter. This type of conversation always made me feel bad. It is more difficult when all the people participating in the conversation are of the same colour, as they do not hold back. When we were returning from the canteen on one occasion, one of the ladies had a word with the lady who was voicing her opinion most strongly and let her know that my husband was coloured, whatever that meant. There are all kinds of colour and race in the world, to say one is coloured could mean anything. Did she mean he was of African, Indian or Chinese descent, or a mixture of any of these? Did she just mean he was not white? After receiving this information she quickened her pace and caught up with me. She said, "I am so sorry. I did not know that your husband was coloured, otherwise I would not have gone on." I said to her, "I would not change my opinion for you. I do not see why you should change yours for me." She was a little taken aback with my rebuke.

I gave a lot of thought to the conversation and came to the conclusion that if the thief was white, I would realise he had nothing to do with me. Just because he was black, why was I so sensitive? Was it a deep inferior complex or prejudice on my part? I talked myself through this dilemma and came to the conclusion that there were bad people in all races. I should be specific: If a person said, a black person was a thief fine, if they said all black people were thieves, then that was prejudice. I was very pleased with my new way of thinking. It freed me from putting too much emphasis on a type of racist conversation. I was happy to reconcile my feelings on this issue.

We all worry about a comment made and spend hours dissecting the meaning. We get sucked into a spiral of negative thought.

This is called over thinking. It starts with a comment, I go over it. Rolling it around in my brain, kneading it like dough. Negative thought can have an effect on your life and wellbeing. The biology of our brain makes it easy to over think. Thoughts and memories are interwoven in an intricate network of association. So a negatives remark may set off a thought process. Most of us have negative memories from the past, a comment, the wind. Bad weather can also trigger negative thoughts. Women seem to think they have to be perfect, set themselves ridiculous high standards and feel responsible for the world's happiness.

To get back on track from negativity. I needed to actively plan things I enjoyed doing and restore my confidence, which works for me. Celebrate the things I do well. To forgive one's fellow man or woman's weaknesses are important to enable one to move on, not so easy to do. That does not mean hurtful remarks were never said. It could also mean forgiving yourself for not being the perfect mother, partner, daughter, sister or friend. I have to be mindful of over thinking and take time out as this leads me on to a path of depression and negativity.

When I was at work I finished my day's tasks at about noon. I needed a more substantial job.

I was always of the opinion; if I had to work I was going to do a good job. Otherwise I would be grieving for my baby and thinking about what I had to do at home. I developed a policy, when I was at work I worked and when I was at home, I was at home and did not think of work. Easier said than done. The lady who said she needed an assistant could have managed to do my job as well as her job; she seemed to have a lot of time on her hands. I was not going to say anything as I needed a job.

It has always been my habit to ask for more work, build my job to be a job I would be happy to come to every working day. If I do not have enough to fill that day. I would ask if I could help a colleague with their work and take over new tasks and build up my job, make it more interesting and more solid as a job.

I worked in the accounts office. There was a girl using a comptometer to calculate invoices, payroll and all accounts calculations, now that work is done by computers. The girl's name was Ruby when I got to know her. I asked her how difficult it was to learn to use the comptometer. Ruby said, "If I can do it any fool can." I took her at her word. She told me to ask the office manager if the company would be willing to send me for training. I asked the manager and expected a refusal. He said he would look into it. The course was three months. He sent me to a comptometer school in Oxford Street, paid for the course, my train fares and subsidence while I was there. I was at the comptometer school for three weeks to learn the basics.

I came back to the office and worked with Ruby, learning the finer points, such as picking up speed, learning the decimals for shillings and pence and half pence in the pound and committing them to memory. She was a quiet girl but very helpful to me. I now had the makings of a career.

Chapter 36

Walk In The Country

I was happy in the flat but when my daughter fell asleep at night I was feeling very lonely and isolated, John worked long hours and on his day off, he liked to meet up with his cousins for a drink in the winter and cricket in the summer. I went to cricket with him but he was playing and I was not a fan of cricket in those days. If the cricket match was held in a nice area of London or in the country I would go for a walk in the leafy suburbs, wander in and out the roads and dream of living in one of those beautiful houses.

The memories of walks with my mother were always called to mind.

My Mammy liked to take a walk. When we came home from school, she would be ready with the pram, to go for a walk down Farranshone, past the park and turn at Hassetts Cross, past the football stadium and out the road past fields with bushes laden with blackberry fruit. There were different seasons, my favourite was late summer when fruit was in season, Mammy would bring cans to pick blackberries. We would go into a field and pick as many as we could, always going for the very black ripe ones bursting with juice. I would be totally lost in the labour of filling my can, to see the rich berries bursting with juice and when the can was filled to overflowing, I would bring them back to Mammy to fill a larger container. No complaints about being tired from the labour were heard by Mammy. It was an adventure, a game running from bush to bush gathering our black gold, then moving on to another field, until Mammy was happy that she had enough. We would then finish our walk home, coming back by the Ennis road. When we got home Mammy would start to make jam for our tea. Mammy's jam was more a compote of fruit as she added baking apple which melted into the jam and at six o' clock the bread was delivered. As well as the milk, we had a cottage loaf and a Pan. Tea was served, golden Ceylon tea in the cup. It was imported by a store in Limerick that specialised in tea, coffee, wines and cheese. As you walked into the store you could smell the aroma of ground coffee. On our plate we would have Galtee cheese, tomatoes, radishes and spring onions or scallions when available. A loaf of sliced bread, a pound of butter on a plate and the blackberry jam on the table. I cannot describe our pleasure as we spread Irish creamery butter on the hot fresh bread and spooned the compote of blackberry jam on top. I can still remember the explosion of taste buds; it is a taste that top restaurants try to achieve unsuccessfully at times. The jam did not last long in our house; it was gone by the end of the meal or breakfast the next morning.

When the weather is moist and warm in the month of August, it is the season for mushrooms. On one of our walks with Mammy we would leave the road and wander around the field. Finding mushrooms was not an easy task. We would have to search every inch of the field, with sharp eyes, looking for the white umbrella tops, hiding in between turfs of green grass.

They were not in every field. Sheep or houses grazing in a field will cultivate the field. The boys would know the field that yielded our treasure. They were a well-kept secret by locals so that they did not get overrun by the likes of us.

Mammy would tell us not to pick the fairy mushrooms, which were red with yellow spots. If we ate them we would die, even though they were very pretty to look at. We steered clear of them. We did not venture to search woodland sites as our knowledge of mushroom was not extensive, or Mammy's. White umbrella mushrooms were the extent of our knowledge.

When it was time to make our way home, our hoard of mushrooms was quite small, but enough. Mammy would make mushroom soup with mushroom, onions, butter, pepper, milk and a spoon of flour to thicken. It was the best. We would dip our freshly delivered bread crowned with creamery butter into the creamy soup.

Sometimes my brother Chris would leave the house early on Sunday morning. He would go to a field that had mushrooms. He would have heard where the best field was. On his return from foraging, Mammy would fry them for breakfast. They were delicious, they had a much stronger flavour than the mushrooms of today, or my taste buds were more acute to taste then. There is something very ancient, even tribal about gathering in the harvest: neighbours helping to celebrate, the rearing of the hay. It is written in our genes foraging for our supper by the wayside, rose-hip to make syrup, blackberries for jam, apple and pears for juices, mushrooms, wild garlic and herbs of mint, thyme and rosemary to flavour our food. We lost the art of gathering. Our forefathers have done this since the beginning of time. Medicine is a gift given from many plants and herbs, Happy is the man who has a garden, field or allotment. Berries that grow on trees along the canal make ink. The needles from the European yew tree are gathered and used in the production of chemotherapy: docetaxel (taxotere), paclitaxel (taxol) from the bark of a pacific yew. Dandelions are diuretics and they are said to cure warts. These are some of the wonders of the world. One by one the children of our house disappeared out the door, to meet friends and play for a short while, before time to come in for the night.

Chapter 37

Old Woman Of The Road

After tea Mammy said we would take a walk, as it was such a lovely evening. We headed out on our usual route to meet up with the Coonagh Road. As we walked along admiring the view, the sun descending in the sky created an orange glow, the smell of asphalt rising off the road after the rays from the day's sun beat down its heat. Horses and their foals were playing in the green fields; cows were chewing the cud, waiting their call to come home for the night. Small stone walls surrounded the fields, hedge growth with their ripe black berries of red and green, wild flowers knapweed, foxglove, oxeye daisy of white and yellow, pink and blue peeping out from the gaps in the undergrowth.

The green acre was on one side, a grass verge used for grazing, or by travellers to park their caravans outside the city borders. We passed a caravan parked on the green, a horse grazing alongside, his coat gleaming rich chocolate brown. Glowing outside the caravan was a little fire to cook with, encased in a ring of stones. The lady was standing behind a half door looking out as we passed. Mammy saluted in the customary way. "Lovely evening, Ma'am," the lady replied. "Lovely evening, thank God."

The lady pushed open the half door, came down the steps of the caravan and got my Mammy's attention. I had the opportunity to look into her caravan without been observed. It was as neat as a pin with everything in its place and a place for everything. There were beautiful China plates on display, a large Waterford glass bowl. There were little lace curtains and pretty check Avoca lamb's wool blankets brightly woven in the north and cushion covers in bright colours. The outside of the caravan had some age, its paint was faded red and green with a brown curved roof, around the door flowers and motifs were painted, which added to its charm

The lady said to Mammy, "My daughters live in England, one has written me a letter. I will have to wait until I meet up with other travellers who could read it to me at the fair, next month." Mammy agreed to read the letter to her. She was anxious to hear how her daughters were doing. Mammy said, "I would be glad to read it to you." We settled down on whatever we could find to sit on while the lady went inside the caravan and got her daughter's letter.

Mammy read her letter, it was well structured and her daughter mentioned little details about her two children and her younger sister, who had joined her and was at night school getting an education. Mammy asked her about her daughter's husband wondering if he was a traveller too. The lady said, "No, my daughter got dressed up one Saturday night to go to a dance in Limerick City and met him. She did not immediately tell him who she was. He fell in love with her and they married. He had a good job in the bank in Limerick and his family were well respected. She would not have been accepted in his family. So they left for England." Many of the younger generation at the time emigrated.

Mammy was concerned that the lady would not see her children and grandchildren.

She told us, "My daughter and children came home for two weeks every year and we travel around the coast of Ireland enjoying the scenery and sea air. We travelled to Kilkee, Lahinch, Ballybunion, Galway and Waterford where they would take the boat back to England." It seemed a wonderful way of life and adventurous holidays, travelling the countryside at their leisure. On their last holiday the younger grand-daughter wanted to go to the toilet and she took her into a field. When she'd finished she wanted to know where the chain was. We all laughed,

I had never thought about the travelling community before meeting the woman of the road. She was not unlike any of my mother's friends although her accent was different. She did not live in a house. Her caravan was her traveller's home; she was a mother who loved her daughters. She was very strong and brave to travel the road on her own. She kept going with the thought of her own tribe, her daughters and grand-daughters. She was comely, dignified and proud. We said our good nights, wished her well and continued on our walk, back to Farranshone for a cup of tea and bed.

Chapter 38

Things Happen In Threes

My aunt's husband's name was Bob. He was an underwater fitter. He worked at Castlebanks, Arnacrusha, County Clare and for a time in Poulaphouca Hydro-electric generating station in County Wicklow around 1952. There were about ten new houses built for staff there, so you would not go so far as to call it a village. There was a shop on the main road where my aunt could do basic shopping. The shop had been there before the houses were built. If she wanted to do a big shop she would go to the next town. My sister and I would go for our school holidays to visit her and Uncle Bob. My Mammy would bring us and stay for two weeks and leave us with our aunt and uncle until we would be brought back, to return to school. There was a clubhouse for the entertainment of the staff. I remember a place where they played table tennis and a wall we would run along and jump off.

The countryside was our playground we would be out after breakfast running in the fields walking in the woods playing with the children from the other houses. We were told not to go near the lake. We would only come home to eat. To me the sun was shining all the time. I would stand looking out of my aunt's kitchen window, at a vast expanse of land, a panoramic view of open countryside. There were no boundaries or houses that I could see. Hares and rabbits were running and playing, racing across the landscape in great numbers.

My aunt had one son, Peter and no girls and she loved all of her sister's children. Eventually we had five girls in our family and two boys. I overheard a conversation between my Mammy and Daddy. It was all about my aunt wanting to adopt me. My Daddy was furious and took it as a slight. "Does she think I cannot provide for my children?" That was the end of that conversation. I was not worried about it as my aunt was at our house every day and I did not know what being adopted entailed.

Before my uncle moved to County Wicklow, on a Sunday night, if my Daddy had a drink with my Uncle Bob, which was a rare occurrence, he would come back to Granny's to walk home with Mammy and I. Daddy would bring a Baby Power, a small Irish whiskey with him for the ladies. My aunt would plead with my Uncle Bob to sing a song for Granny. He would stand by the fire with all of us seated around. He had a very impressive countenance. Tall with silver grey hair, smiling deep blue eyes, very handsome and he sang in a beautiful tenor voice. He would sing 'Bless this house, O Lord we pray' and 'Silver threads among the Gold" after much applause and praise. My Daddy would sing for Mammy, 'There's a little white cot winding over the hill where two eyes of blue come smiling through.' This was because Granny, Mammy and my Aunt Kay all had very blue eyes. I could have sat there in a warm fuzzy daze all night listening to and enjoying the chat and the songs. My peace was broken by Daddy saying it was getting late and we'd better make a move. We would get our coats and say our goodbyes.

While on holidays in County Wicklow we had an unexpected visit from Daddy who was driving his friend and his wife to Dublin to pick up their son who was in a special school there. Daddy took the opportunity to come and see his children, after his visit we all went to wave him off. Aunt Kay sprinkled holy water from the font in the hall on him. As he was going she said, "God Bless, have a safe journey home."

When they left, the children ran down the hill and over the fields to the clubhouse. We started to play games and some of us ran along the wall and jumped off. I could not remember if I panicked got dizzy or thought that the children were coming too fast behind me. I let myself go and fell, I could not remember anything until I woke up some time later. I was bleeding from my ear and the doctor was there. He said I had cracked the drum of my ear. I had to stay in bed and have drops for my ear. He would come back to see how I was in a few days. They asked me if I had been pushed. I said no I had just fallen.

After a few days I begged to go out and play, I was so bored, I could see and hear the children running and playing from my bedroom window. I was allowed to go out for so long as they all watched out for the doctor and warned me so I could run back indoors and hop in to bed. Sure enough one of the children saw his car coming down the road; I ran back and was still panting when he came up the stairs. My Uncle Bob would regularly call me to test my hearing. I thought it was funny because his finger was so big, it did not cover my good ear properly. His voice boomed when he called my name to check my hearing and asked me if I heard. Of course I did. I would say yes and be allowed to go and play.

On the same day that I had my fall my Mammy was cycling in Limerick City with my younger sister Helen sitting in the basket seat at the back of the bicycle. All of a sudden Mammy was aware of people on the pavement who were trying to get her attention. Helen had caught her foot in the spokes of the bicycle wheel. My Mammy was devastated to think she was responsible for injuring her own child, I do not think she ever got over it. My sister had to go to hospital and spend some time there She developed cysts on the back of her neck maybe from the shock; they burst the morning they planned to operate. I remember when we came back from our holiday in Dublin my sister Helen was crawling on the floor. She had to learn to walk again. Mammy was always very sensitive to her needs as she was small in size and Mammy carried a lot of guilt about her accident. Mammy came home after leaving Helen at the hospital in those days. Mothers were not encouraged to stay with their children, they thought it would be unsettling for them; I am glad that has changed. Helen remembers standing up in an iron cot looking out of the window at the river hoping and longing for Mammy to come for her. They did not allow visitors for children in hospital at that time.

Mammy told me that she was sitting at the table crying over Helen when our neighbour came and knocked on the door. She came to see if she could comfort Mammy about Daddy's accident, Mammy did not know. She told her that Daddy had a car accident outside Dublin. She had heard it on the news. Mammy had the radio turned off. If all was well she would have the radio on, she always listened to the news; you daren't make any noise when it was on. Daddy was not injured but the lady in the back seat was. I always thought that my aunt splashing holy water on Daddy had saved him. The accident was caused by the driver of the other car, bottles of drink were found on the floor by the guards. I was sorry that the accidents were not timed. It seemed to me that the accidents happened around the same time. It would have been interesting to compare the timing.

Chapter 39

My Sister's Illness

J ohn and I did our shopping on Saturday morning. We worked out the finances thus: I paid for the groceries out of my wages; he would buy the fruit and a chicken. I paid the nanny to mind the baby and there was none left. John gave me the money to save and the rent. That is how we saved enough money for the deposit for the house. John was careful with money. He sent some to his mother in Trinidad and his sister in Grenada, who had a large family. His sister wrote to him and told him about an acre of land that was for sale. She told him to buy it; it could be a very good investment for him. Land in Grenada was expensive; he bought the acre. He sent money to pay for it every month. I would go to the bank and deposit what was left into his account.

My daughter Louise, being an only child, got a toy every week. I got a cardboard barrel with a lid and wallpapered the outside. I would say Daddy is coming home and she would put her toys into the barrel when she finished playing. I was very comfortable and felt settled in the flat. It felt like home. The kitchen was large enough to wash clothes, iron and have all our meals. I could spend all my time there when I was not working. When we went to Woolworth's on Saturday, Louise got a little toy, I was afraid she was getting spoilt. I wanted to have another baby. John did not want any more children as he saw large families as poverty. He was forward thinking and perhaps he understood, we did not have a home of our own. It would have made it easier if he talked to me more about how he felt. In the end he agreed. When the landlady saw I was pregnant she said we would have to move out while they renovated the flat.

When I was six months' pregnant my sister Phillis's tubercular glands in her stomach flared up again. She was hospitalised. She had it while she was nursing and was treated but had to leave nursing as it was too arduous for her. The recurrence of TB was probably due to poor living conditions, living in one room with two children. She had the second one very soon after the first. She was a hard worker. My sister Phillis had an abundance of energy. She could make a clean sweep of her room and have everything shining in no time. I had to clean as I went as my energy levels were not so high. She was looking after my daughter at the time and when I came from work to pick Louise up; Phillis told me that she had fallen asleep in the chair. When she woke up, the children had emptied the contents of the food press on to the floor to make a cake. There was flour, sugar, milk and butter spread all over the floor, as well as in their hair, clothes and hands. Some days later she woke to see the same thing again, this time she said my daughter was sitting at the other end of the room, having nothing to do with it. I was worried about her sleeping; it was not like her, as she was always on the go. She went into hospital soon after that.

I told John that I would have to bring my sister's children home to Ireland to my mother. He agreed and I handed in my notice at work, so that I could take her children and my daughter to Ireland to my mother. Mammy would help look after Phillis's children, until she recovered. Phillis's eldest son Paul was three weeks older than my daughter Louise and her daughter Anna was two years younger. It was a long and arduous journey with me six months pregnant with two three-and-a-half-year-olds and a two-year-old. Getting the baby's bottle sterilised and her bottles of milk on the train and boat was not straightforward. I got a cabin on the boat and put the children to sleep. When we arrived at the dock I was sorry to have to wake the babies to disembark and get the train to Limerick.

When I got to Limerick Junction I washed and changed the children into new clothes, so that their grandparents could see them in their best, looking so beautiful, as they were. They were very good children, it was a hard journey with me pregnant. Years later my niece said her Mom was very upset when they were reunited. She heard her daughter call me Mom. I did not know, she would have heard my daughter call me Mom and copied her. I was to stressed dealing with the forthcoming birth of my son and the threats of losing my flat.

Chapter 40

Birth Of Baby Boy

I had a beautiful baby boy after a difficult birth. He was 21 ins long and over nine lbs. I carried him for over ten months. He was very overdue. I was in the maternity hospital a month before and came out on the 8th April. They tried for a week to induce me, but it didn't work. They told me that when I walked around at home, I may be straight back. Every week I saw the same doctor, but on the fourth week I saw a different doctor. He said, "I know you." I told him about being induced and he was one of the doctors who saw me. He wanted me to be admitted straight away. I said no, I had to pick up my daughter from the childminder. I had left my daughter with the childminder, so I came into the hospital the next morning. I was induced and I started straight away. When John came from work, he came to see me. I told the nurse to tell him to come back tomorrow. I heard the nurse say, 'Go in and cheer your wife up.' I was in such pain, I was very annoyed with the nurse. I told John to come back in the morning and he did.

We were both very proud of our family. My son was a big boy and looked like a four-month baby when he was born. His skin was very dry and I had to rub him down in baby oil, all the time.

On the Sunday after we brought my son home from the hospital, we had a visit from John's school friend early in the morning. He was standing over the carry cot, which was on a stand in our bedroom, admiring baby Allen and laughing with John. They were delighted with the arrival of the first male in our family. Men seem to feel that their name will carry on into the future with the male child. The woman will marry and take her husband's name.

He was saying what a fine boy he was and such a big boy. My daughter was asleep in her cot beside them, or so they thought. She was lying in her cot with her eyes closed.

The men left the bedroom and had coffee in the kitchen. I went into the bedroom to wake Louise, get her to the bathroom and get her washed and dressed. She had a high fever and had red spots. I checked behind her ears. I called John to come and look at her and he said "call the doctor!" When the doctor came he diagnosed measles. I told the doctor that she had the measles before, she could not have them again. He said it could have been a fever before and not the measles. I kept the blinds down to protect her eyes.

I had to go to the shop on our road; an elderly neighbour was leaning on her gate, arms folded. She asked me, "What did you have love, a boy or girl? How did it go?" I told her about my son, I told her he was fine and that my daughter had measles. The doctor had just left. I said, "I don't understand it, she had the measles before." She said, "It will not be the measles, she will be upset about the baby, just make a fuss of her and it will go." When I returned I told John. He went into the bedroom and took her out of her cot and carried her to the kitchen. He put her on his knee and fed her little tit-bits from his breakfast plate. He chatted with her all the time. We never mentioned the measles and when I looked later that day they had disappeared.

She had been our only child for a long time, it was hard on her. Louise felt she was losing her place in the family and our love. That could never happen. I remembered John having a very bad toothache in the same week. I said to let me see. When I looked he was getting a wisdom tooth. I was getting one that week and Louise was also teething. He would not believe me and went to the dentist to have an extraction, only to be told he was getting his wisdom teeth. He was given painkillers.

Mrs Fernandez, our landlady, said they were going to Spain on holiday and would I mind the dog. I said yes. As soon as they arrived back Mr Fernandez said, "You have to move, as I need to do the windows and do up the whole flat." It did not need doing up. John said, "We could move into one room while the work is being done on the other." He said, "No, the furniture has to be moved into the other rooms." John offered, "I will come after work to help you, so that it's done quickly and we can move back in." The next day when John went to the house after work, Mr Fernandez changed the locks on the door and said he did not want children living in the house. We were now evicted.

Chapter 41

My Son's Christening

The day came when it was time for my son to be christened, so I made my way to a newly built RC church in Stonebridge called The Five Precious Wounds. I spoke to the priest's housekeeper; she was in the presbytery, a house attached to the church, in Harlesden. She told me to bring Allen on Sunday after 12pm Mass. I asked, "Do I need to bring any documentation?" She said, "No need, just come with the baby and godparents." John and I went with Louise and Allen to visit my sister Phillis and her husband David and their two children. I told them the arrangements for our son's baptism. I asked my sister and her husband to be godparents. They agreed. Then John said, "We have nowhere to invite people to come after the baptism." It was true we were moving, from room to room after our eviction from Harley Road. We were waiting on news of our mortgage with regards to the purchase of our new house. John said, "I cannot go, If I do not go to cricket on Sunday my cousins will work out I am having Allen christened." They will say, 'You have to give a party.' He said, "It is not possible at present. All the money I have has to go towards the house." This was the first I heard of him not coming, it is true we were in very poor housing conditions at the time. The cricket team consisted mainly of John's cousins and the husbands of cousins. There would be strong opposition to him not having a party. They would have thought it was their duty to persuade him to celebrate.

They did not know we were getting a house as John was a private person. They would not have guessed that he had saved the money for the deposit, £1,100. It was saved by hard work and no frills in our life. He would not say anything as he thought if he talked about it, it would not happen. You could say why did I not wait until we got the house for Allen to be baptised.

Getting the house seemed a distant dream. I did not believe that it would happen.

David, Phillis's husband, said to John, "Don't worry John, Phillis and I will take Marie and the children to the church." It was a very stressful time for me with the pressure of moving and living in very poor housing, so I bowed to their superior knowledge. Phillis or David did not see anything was wrong with John's decision or try to persuade him to go to the church. On the Sunday John brought me, Louise and Allen to David and Phillis's house and left. So off John went to cricket and I went with Phillis, David and their two children, together with Louise and Allen to the church. We were all dressed in our finery, a new dress and new shoes and socks for Louise, my son looking very good in his white baby suit and shawl. Louise's long hair was tied with a white ribbon.

We arrived at the church, all was new and splendid. The priest seemed to be a little disappointed with our arrival. I felt the other parents were special to him, he may have intended for the baptism of their baby to be celebrated on its own. He appeared to be very close to the other parents and in deep conversation with them.

His housekeeper did not inform him about our small party. The priest spoke to my brother-in-law and asked if he was the father. He said no he was the godfather and he did not offer any explanation. I felt embarrassed; it looked as if I was a single parent. The priest continued talking to the other parents.

After the baptism we went back to my sister's house and had tea and a christening cake...I have always regretted not having the sense or knowledge to communicate to John how important the baptism of my son was to me. I just accepted a lot of what was dished out in those days I was twenty-two in April 1967 and Allen was born in May 1967. I came from a Catholic background and I would not have to explain had I married someone from home. I thought that was how things were when you married someone from a foreign country. Later on I saw the West Indian ladies in action and I realised that they were very strong. They would never accept their husband going to a cricket match on the day their son got baptised, party or no party. This then made me feel very inadequate.

People are people; there are no excuses for different cultures behaving differently. Whatever the ceremony carried out after birth, humans have always had a very important ceremony. After seven days Hindus shaved the baby's head, Jews and Muslims circumcise, Sikhs have a naming ceremony. It is a welcome into the culture and religious beliefs of their people.

Chapter 42

Day By The Sea

Another sunny summer day and cricket. I had long been asking John to go to the seaside for the day. We could not afford a holiday. He was happy playing cricket with his family. I was not. I longed to see the sea. I told John I was not going to cricket. I was getting a train to the seaside. He agreed and on Sunday morning, John and his cousin brought Louise and baby Allen and me to the train station and put us on a train to Bournemouth. I was a little worried about getting off the train with the pushchair and the bags full with Allen's nappies bottles etc . . . I managed, we arrived and made our way to the sea. We had arranged for John to meet us at six o' clock that evening.

Louise and I had ice creams and we headed towards the beach. I told Louise that she could play on the sand with her bucket and spade. I took her shoes and socks off and put her on the sand. She cried, she did not like the feel of the sand on her feet. So I had to clean the sand off and put her shoes and socks back on, pack up the pushchair and leave the beach. We walked along the promenade and sat on the benches looking out at the blue sea and sky. The bucket and spade I bought for Louise was wasted, she was not interested in the sand. She was a tidy, little girl always pulling her socks up.

I put Allen on my lap and while he slept, my mind wandered back to my youth and a holiday in Kilkee.

My family was large, nine of us in all, including my parents. When we were young and there were less of us, we would go on holidays in the summer to Kilkee. Daddy would hire a car to take us there. After much preparation, we would set off. I remember one year my grandmother bought my sister, my brother and I red blazers, Black Watch tartan pleated skirt for the girls and my brother grey trousers. Little lemon short-sleeved jumpers for us girls.

Mammy always bought Clark sandals at the start of the summer and brown shoes at the beginning of the school year. She would say, "I do not want to see any scuff marks on your new shoes." It was virtually impossible for children, for the first ten minutes I would be very careful how I walked and then play took over and I forgot. Even though I was young, I sat in the back seat of a large car. I knew I looked nice with my new white socks and sandals, my blazer, pleated skirt and lemon jumper.

We headed off to Kilkee to stay at a cottage on the sea front, run by the Ms Keans. My aunt, uncle and cousin would arrive around the same time. The excitement grew as my Mammy took some time to get organised with the pram and the younger children. We changed into our summer dresses and headed to the beach stopping along the way for a red shiny bucket with seaside scenes and a spade for the sand. I looked longingly at the wind mill as it spun around in the breeze with its kaleidoscope of colour. To ask for it as well, was pushing my luck.

Mammy and my aunt would make themselves comfortable on the blanket, laid on the beach.

We were free to roam the beach, go in groups or wander off, with warnings, "Be careful on the rocks, the moss is slippery, do not fall in to the sea." I would examine the pools trapped between the rocks for little crabs, tiny fish, periwinkle and other small shellfish clinging to the rocks. I spent hours roaming and investigating those pools, running back to Mammy , if I thought I could get an ice cream. I was running in and out of the waves, looking for shells to put in my bucket, until we were called to dinner.

The Ms Keens laid a very good table with soup tureen and all the serving dishes. Filled with soup, streaming potatoes and vegetables I thought their food was good. After a morning playing, swimming and investigating the wildlife, I would be ravenous.

Now the Ms Keens had rules and they were told to us on our arrival. Their strictest rules were about sand. We were not to come into their house with sand on our feet. A bucket of water and a towel were placed outside, by the kitchen door. We had to wash our feet before we came indoors. There were times when I ran indoors, to get something I had forgotten, without washing my feet and I was severely reprimanded.

Mammy and my aunt used to invite friends, twin brothers from Dublin, to join them for a short holiday; they stayed at a large hotel. They were identical twins the same as Mammy and my aunt. I thought at the time that they were a little effeminate. They loved to be seen with Mammy and my aunt as the two sets of twins got a lot of attention. Daddy and my uncle treated them like family.

I cherish the memories of standing on the beach, looking at the vast Atlantic Sea with blue skies and blue waves tipped with white surf rolling in over the sand. Cliffs of green and the grey slated rock pools nestled beneath the cliffs on either side of the beach.

When you are young everything is in Technicolour and very large. I would stand on the beach and take in the panoramic view, which I never tired of. On our visits back to the blanket and Mammy we would sometimes be given sixpence for a pint of periwinkle which we shared. The pint cup being the measuring cup and three pence for a bag of dullish, which we would eat with relish. You will still find a lady selling periwinkle and dullish on the Kilkee promenade in the summer months.

The sun did not always shine and I can remember it raining for an eternity while I looked out the window at the wind and rain creating havoc with the sea. My aunt came to the window and had us sing. 'Rain, rain, go away come again another day.'. The next day the sun shone. We were out the door after breakfast as we knew our way around by now, so we did not have to wait on Mammy.

All good things come to an end. We would leave the beautiful sea and return to our home as the summer holidays were coming to a close. We had to prepare for our return to school and move into our new class one up hopefully. On our first day, came the essay we were required to write: What I did on my summer holiday. Teacher or nun would point to the picture on the classroom wall, of a day by the sea.

What was missing with our day at the sea with my children, was family, cousins for the children to play with, aunts and uncles. Louise and I were hungry and we headed in the direction of the cafe for tea and snacks. I asked them to heat milk for Allen and his jar of dinner which they kindly did. Then we headed back to the train station. As we slowly pulled into Victoria station I saw John waiting for us on the platform.

Chapter 43

First Days Of School

On my sister Phillis's first day at school. I recall Mammy pushing the pram with my brother Chris in it, me holding on to the pram and Phillis dressed in her new School uniform and blazer, looking very smart and grown up with her blonde hair shining and tied up in a white ribbon. Through the school gate we went. The school yard was deserted. Mammy could have been late which I recall was a usual occurrence when I had to go to school. More than likely the times when pupils were accepted into school on their first day were staggered. At the door to the school stood a nun dressed in black, resembling a large blackbird with a thin pale face, long and serious. Phillis started to cry building up to a crescendo, clinging to Mammy. Sister said, "We do not tolerate this kind of behaviour." She firmly grasped my sister's hand, turned and went inside; she left us standing at the entrance to the school. Mammy burst into tears and cried all the way home. Phillis was the first of our family to go to school. Mammy was devastated at having to let her go to a perfect stranger. My recollection was "I will not cry when I have to go to school." We did not come home from school at lunchtime during the early years. We would bring a small bottle of milk and a sandwich in our school bags, which had to be eaten at lunchtime. My grandfather liked to tease Phillis. He would say, "I will bring your dinner over to the school at lunchtime, you can eat it at your desk, a nice plate of bacon and cabbage." She would plead with tears in her eyes. "Grand-dad please, please do not bring my dinner to school." He would smile and chuckle. Had I been asked I would have been happy to have him bring my dinner, but I was never asked.

Time moved on and it was my turn to go to school. Mammy was not taking any chances with me. When she saw the nun at the door she promptly handed me over and turned and walked away and back home. There were two children younger than me and another on the way. She had a lot to do and would be glad of one less child to deal with; she could get on with her work. She had plenty to do at home. On my first day at school after prayers we had to learn the Irish for "do I have your permission to leave the room, please?" before you could go to the toilet. Sister would repeat it with you when you put your hand up. I remember saying it over and over when I urgently needed to go. It was the quickest I have ever learned anything. That night I wanted my bottle of milk to go to sleep as I was still having a bottle at night. My Mammy came into my room and said, "What would Sister Mary say if she knew you still had a bottle." She put her hand out. I handed over the bottle and that was the last I saw of it.

I was asked on many occasions why I was late for school. I would not reply. If I said it was my Mammy's fault there would be a comment from Sister, she would make my Mammy look bad. I would be in a loss situation whatever I said so I said nothing. Sister would send me to the back of the class to stand up for the rest of the lesson. Mammy could not be blamed in my eyes as she had young babies to feed, clean and get ready to walk to school with me. I would not have Sister thinking she was not a good mother.

My teacher in middle school was Ms McCarthy. She had a favourite in the class He had black, curly, hair, beautiful eyes and she smiled at him a lot and asked him if he was all right. She sat him at the front desk near her. The School Inspector visited us, as he did unexpectedly once a year, when he left. Ms McCarthy opened her handbag and took out her powder and lipstick and re applied it, saying to her favourite, 'I must look awful.' He nodded no. He was a quiet boy and never said much. Her favouritism isolated him from the class children. One day her favourite sat on the edge of his bench and the other end came down on her toes. She cried and said she never thought he would do that to her. I was shocked at the injustice. It was an 'accident' I wanted to say to her. He hadn't done it on purpose.

One Friday after lunch we were brought in to another class room to different activities. I found myself in a corner and to my joy playing with bricks, making houses and building things. I was lost to all around me, concentrating on building something. It was not coming out like I wanted it to. I would try again and again. I was very disappointed when the bell rang and we had to leave and go home. I can still remember the wonderful feeling of trying to create an object. We were never taken there again. I can only think that our teacher had to leave early and we were given an occupation with an understudy. I wished it happened again I never forgot the deep sense of satisfaction at being totally absorbed in a task and oblivious to the world.

One day I was taken out of the classroom. It was coming up towards Christmas and the school play and concert was coming up. Another girl was there also, she was around my age. The nuns wanted us to walk up some steps on the stage, with the bigger girls holding night lights at either side of each step. It was supposed to be Our Lady going to the Temple as a young child to be educated. The nuns picked the other girl to do the part and she cried all the way up the steps, so they sent her back to her class. I walked the steps slowly as told by Sister and did not see a necessity to cry as I did not fully grasp the situation. There would be parents watching me in a live performance. That is how I was picked.

It did not bother me when I had to perform, as the Nuns took me from a classroom to the side stage and told me to walk the steps. I walked on and up the steps with the bigger girls lined up on either side. This time their lamps were lit and there was a golden glow. I was dressed in a long, white, satin dress with a blue sash. I walked slowly up one side and down the other side, off the stage. On the other side a Sister walked me back to the classroom passing a picture that always fascinated me, of a girl crossing over a ravine on a rope bridge surrounded by forest with rushing waters running through the ravine. She was safe for her guardian angel was with her.

My Mammy took me home as it was a night performance and past my bedtime. I did not see the audience as I walked in because of the glow from the lamps. The play was on for two nights. The next night Sister was getting me ready in my satin dress and there was a scratch on my face. I was interrogated as to how it happened. I said the cat did it, my sister and I had a fight that day. Sister said tell the cat if I see her, I will have words with her.

Chapter 44

Red Blazers

My sister Phillis and I went off to school wearing the red blazers Granny bought us. We looked very smart. We must have pleaded with Mammy to wear them. They were not the school uniform. It was the month of May. The nuns would not have seen our blazers, if we kept then out of their view.

When we hung them in the cloakroom we did not make it too obvious, that we were not wearing our correct uniform, a navy cardigan or school blazer over a pale blue dress white round collar and six mother-of-pearl little buttons in twos at the front of the dress. At the end of the school day the bell rang and school was out.

My sister and a friend met me outside the school gate. It was decided that we would go over the wall and in to the woods across from the school. We let the other children drift home, while we hung back.

The Christian Brothers owned the woods. They lived in a clearing; in a large white house. The forest was magic. It was a hot day so we left our blazers under a tree. It was the season for bluebells; the forest floor was a carpet of different shades of blue, some verging on pink and some white. We walked through the forest, with an eye on the big white house, watching out for any stray monks or priests.

I saw a young monk walking from the main house to the out buildings. I was nervous, but he seemed very far away. If he came near us, we would have to make our way to the wall and jump down on the pavement. The drop to the road was longer on the outside of the wall, than in the forest, we would move quickly if we saw a monk approach.

We were lost in wonderment at the beauty of trees, many shapes and sizes, years older than us. We looked at the old trees, with their high branches and gnarled bark. My sister and her friend walked on. I sat under a tree where the sunlight filtered through the leaves, surveying the beauty of my surroundings and enjoying the subtle scent of bluebells. I was in a trance with the beauty of it all. I do not know how long I spent there, mesmerised, or at what point I saw the monk heading in my direction. He was close. The alarm went out, we ran as if our lives depended on it. Over the wall we tumbled and ran home. When we got to our road we realised that we had left our red blazers in the woods. We could not go back and ask for their return as the woods were out of bounds. We would have to hide the fact, that we lost our blazers from Mammy, at least for a day or two.

Next morning all classes went to school prayers in the school hall. A class at a time moved in orderly procession up the hall under the gaze of a picture of the Guardian Angel. The hall filled up. Nuns and teachers stood in a line across the hall, backs to the wall, keeping their eye on us. All the classes were present. Prayers were said, led by Mother Superior standing elevated on the stage. She stood and looked with piercing eyes into the faces of children in the hall. She produced the red blazers that were sitting on a small table behind her. I had not noticed them. She said, "I have an announcement to make," holding our red blazers up in full view. "These two red blazers were handed in to the convent by the Christian Brothers. Will the children who own them collect them from my office." I did not own up to the loss, at that time. I briefly saw my sister Phillis at break time. She said, "I am not going for the blazers; you go." At that point I did not think that Phillis is older than me, she should go. I was torn between the devil and the deep blue sea: the Reverend Mother or Mammy. After some time I raised enough courage to approach the Reverend Mother's office. I knew I had to get back the red blazers. Someone in my class may tell the nuns they were ours. I knocked softly on the Mother Superior's door. I heard the command "Come in!" I was now trapped in a web. She looked at me, sternly, waiting. "I have come for the red blazers, Reverend Mother," I said. I was given the two blazers after a stern lecture from Mother Superior about trespassing on the Christian Brothers' property. I felt the horror of the monks having to knock on the nun's door. I looked duly repentant and said, "I will not go there again, Mother Superior." My stress levels returned to normal as I escaped from her office. Life went back to normal.

Chapter 45

The Terror Of Being In Trouble

When I was young my Mammy would say, "You were sleepwalking again last night." I was unaware of it. I would not believe what she said. Mammy would say, "You tried to climb up the wall again last night, "there was a small alcove near the ceiling." I would have stepped from the bed on to the mantelshelf and tried to go further. I asked Mammy what happened then. She said, "I told you to come down, go back to bed, go to sleep." It seemed a very strange thing to do. Mammy explained, "If someone is sleepwalking, you just tell them to go back to bed. It is not good to wake them up." I believe these incidents happened when I was concerned about something, or when I was in trouble at school or in family life. This would be the time when I was worried about an incident that happened at my aunt's.

Across from the People's park in Pery Square, was my father's family home. When the men of the house got married and left home, the aunts converted the house into a small hotel. My aunty asked my father if I could spend a week with them, as there was a young girl my age staying there with her aunts. They were in a show called 'The Terry Golden Show." It was showing at a theatre in Limerick. My friend did Irish dancing early in the show and when she finished she was brought back to my aunt's, where I was waiting. We spent the rest of the evening chatting. We had great fun, laughing, playing and reading together. We became good friends.

At that time my aunt had regular boarders, who worked in Limerick. Their homes were in other counties in Ireland. They stayed at my aunt's during the week and returned to their homes at the weekends. Two of the regulars guests were often in the kitchen, chatting. One was a small man, who had black, curly hair and played the violin. He was a gifted player. I enjoyed listening to him play Irish traditional tunes, with ease. He was a very nice, quiet man. The second was a fair, tall, good looking man, with charisma.

He was in the kitchen one day during my stay and my friend started to call his name, teasing him and running away. I thought this was good sport and joined in. At first he just made a noise at us. Then he gave chase, he ran after us up the stairs and into the large dining room, on the first floor. I cannot remember what we were saying to him, just childish nonsense. He grabbed me and sat on a chair, pulled up my clothes and spanked me. I was so humiliated. He let me go, I was livid. To say I saw red was an understatement. My father had never laid hands on me.

All I remember was that I saw a box of matches sitting on the entrance hall table and I grabbed them and said to my friend, "I am going to set fire to his car." He had an old Morris Minor. We ran out to the car. I was so angry and ashamed. I knew I was acting the bravado. I did not think for one moment, striking a match and holding it in through the window of the car, was going to set the car on fire. As I held the match between my fingers, a whisper of blue flames crossed the felt roof at lightning speed and the car started to smoke. I patted the roof with my hand to stop the blue flame. I screamed at my friend, "Tell him his car was on fire "and I took off at high speed. I went home and lived in terror.

I knew my father called on his sisters for his elevenses every day, during the week. I felt that the aunts discussed it and thought secretly that it was a just punishment, for laying hands on their niece.

He was taking his girlfriend to the seaside that day. He was furious as he complained to my aunts, that the car smoked all day on his journey to the seaside and back. Needless to say, I was terrified to visit my aunts, in case I ran in to him.

Daddy never mentioned it to Mammy. I was very relieved, as I would have the third degree from Mammy. She would have been very angry with me for being familiar with a man, who was staying at my aunts, or any man come to that. I knew I did wrong by setting his car on fire.

My troubles did not end there. When I was in town shopping for Mammy, he spotted me walking on one of the pavements of William Street or O' Connell Street while cruising in his car. I took off running up and down the streets and back alleys in terror, with him revving up his car and giving chase, following me in the car, up one road and down another. I found an escape route, if I ran up the alley behind Woolworth's, I could run through the shop and come out on the main street, cross the road and run down to the river Shannon and later go home when the coast was clear.

These events had me very troubled. I lived in fear that he would catch me. I lived in terror of what he would do.

Eventually he got married to the girl in the car; his employer transferred him to another town. I was rid of him for good. I could now breathe a sigh of relief. I now feel on reflection that he would cruise up and down the streets searching for me in his free time looking to take his revenge.

Later on when I was in trouble at school I developed a rasping cough. It may have been asthma. My father brought me to his company doctor which was the first time in my life, since I was born, that I had been to a doctor. I was amazed that the doctor should try to cure me of my cough when he had a severe twitch on the side of his face, he was not able to cure that. He asked me if I smoked. I thought this man is mad: why would I smoke? I was eleven-years-old. I said no and we left the surgery. I think my father was not impressed. When I lay down to sleep at night, I would get a fit of coughing. I could hear my Daddy say from his chair, "She will end up in the city home, mark my words." This was a hospital at the top of our road for TB and contagious diseases. I got over my cough and, after some months, I returned to school.

Now you are thinking what was she up to in school that caused the trouble? Well, my friend Alesha had an autograph book and asked me to sign it, as she did to all of the class. I wrote

The higher the mountain,
The cooler the breeze,
The younger the couple,
The tighter, the squeeze.

Now if you asked me where I heard this, it was probably in the playground, or the road. I could not tell you anything other than the direct translation of the words. The Reverend Mother read more into it than me. Alesha's autograph book was confiscated by the nuns in the playground; they regarded it as the devil's work. We were called into the head nun's office, one by one. Some of the girls had written:

Roses are red

Violets are blue

Sugar is sweet

And so are you.

They were not in as much trouble as me. My turn came. I was told, "You are not only a bad example on your class but a bad example on the school as a whole." Mammy and Alesha's mother were sent for. Alesha was sent to an agricultural boarding college and I never saw her again. Her mother was from the country. She ran a poultry farm.

Mammy was told by Sister, to remove me from the school. Mammy told her she had no money to send me to a boarding school. I saw Mammy's face as she came down the steps that led to our garden and to our house. She was in a foul mood and needless to say I was in big trouble.

Sister said that as punishment I had to go every Saturday morning to the convent to do tests. Sister put me in to their visitors' room that was actually very nice. I loved it, highly polished floor and furniture, a beautiful wooden table and seat for me to sit at to do my work and their beautiful grounds to look out on, if Sister delayed coming back. The room across the hall had a beautiful tiny chapel, which I had a peek at. The convent was a very private place; the students did not get further than the front door. I reasoned if she asked me why I left the room I would say I was looking for her. I had finished my work.

She would give me a maths paper to do. I would do it and wait on her return. She never said if they were correct. She would take them and tell me come back the next Saturday. I rather enjoyed it and did not think of it as a punishment. After some time she told me, "You need not come any more." I am glad to say the sleepwalking stopped.

Chapter 46

Physiology

I managed to get through the next few years without much fuss. One sunny day in sixth form, I was looking out the window of the classroom. I saw the boats coming up the Shannon river to Limerick, which is sixty miles up from the sea and has a port. It is the last deep water the boat meets at low tide on its journey up the mouth of the Shannon.

The Sister teaching me at the time was very nice; she was one of a family of three related sisters in the community. I liked her, she was interesting and pleasant. I still lived my policy of non-co-operation, though I was never rude at school. I would rather play the game; I was not the full shilling. Sister spotted me dreaming. She addressed the class, "Marie does not have to do any work in this class, she does not have to do any homework, she can sit and look out the window for the rest of the term." I thought this arrangement suited me very well. She was using psychology on me.

I enjoyed my time for a day or two and then I got bored. I started to do my homework but I never handed it in and she never asked for it. One day she had a visitor knock on the door. She addressed the class, "Please do not make any noise while I am out of the class, open your books and read the next chapter." Chaos erupted when she left but I knew she meant what she said. She came back into the class and she was not happy. She told the class to open their history books and learn the next chapter by heart. That consisted of a page and a half. The class did not take her seriously. I knew she meant what she said. I learned it by heart that night. In the morning after prayers, she addressed the first girl in the row and went through the class with no success. She looked at me in desperation and said, "Is there any hope of asking you" I stood up and was halfway through it before her mouth was able to move and she said, "OK, that is enough. Sit down!"

Soon after that we did our primary certificate and entrance to the secondary. When the results came we had to go to the head nun's office to receive our certificate or receive the results with a pep talk. My class teacher came to me and said, "What are you going to do with your life?" I said I would go to England; my sister had gone when she was sixteen and became a cadet nurse. My Mammy's cousin was a nun in a nursing hospital in Wales. Sister told me it was my turn to go to the head's office. I knocked and entered. The head nun was tall, thin with a sallow complexion. She started with, "Of all the children in this school you are the least deserving." I do not know what the rest of the conversation was about, I was not listening, I knew I had made it...

Chapter 47

College Park Scrubs Lane

After our eviction from our flat in Harley Road John and his cousin moved us to a room in a house in College Park, it was not good. It was a room in a West Indian family home. John was working nights. It was very frightening. The first night I settled my two children and fell asleep. After midnight there was a great commotion, the mother shouting at the children to go to bed. Then at six in the morning she was beating the child who wet the bed.

I got my children ready and went to the shops. As I was leaving I spoke to a young girl, a daughter of the house. She was kept home from school to look after her sister's baby. I went out, did my shopping and as I was coming back, I saw smoke coming from under their sitting room door. I knocked at the door; the girl did not open it, so I banged on the door and said, "I will break this door down if you do not open it." While this was going on I had to leave my babies outside the front door. She eventually opened the door. She had lit some paper on the gas stove in the kitchen as a lighter for the paraffin fire. Bits of the lighting paper dropped, creating little fires across the carpet, It then caught alight with a series of small fires. I helped her to put the fires out, she got carpet shampoo and tried to do the best she could to hide the burn marks. She was terrified her mother would find out. When her mother came home from work she went straight into the kitchen. When her Dad came in from work, he sat down in front of the TV; under his foot was a big burn on the carpet. I passed the young girl in the hall on my way to the kitchen. I looked at her expectantly, she nodded that they had not seen the burn marks.

The next day after seeing the house agent, I arrived back at the house and there were two policemen at the door and a great deal of explaining by the mother. It appeared the son had taken her gold watch and swapped it for marbles in the school yard. It was brought to the attention of the head teacher. She returned it to the eldest daughter, to give to her mother. The mother beat the boy. He screamed the house down and the neighbour called the police. The police were happy with the explanation and went on their way calling it a domestic. As they went the boy said to the mother, "If you hit me again, the police will hold you and lock you up."

I met the mother some time later in the market; I asked her how her family was. She told me the boy was at boarding school. I was amazed and said that must be very expensive. She said, "No, it did not cost anything. I just had to go to court and tell them, I could not manage him."

I told John we had to move again. He moved us to another room, the landlord and his wife had separated. The wife did not want to give us the room, as she feared what her husband would say. John knew him. It was the house he had come to when he first came to England. His family had all moved to better accommodation. He told her we were waiting for completion on the purchase of a house we were buying. It would be temporary; John would talk to him when he came to collect the rent at the weekend.

I was on my own with the children. They were fast asleep when I heard fireworks going off. I opened the conservatory door to the garden. It was Guy Fawkes Night.

I did not know what day it was before that, all the days merged into one. I looked up at the sky to see a burst of light, as a display of fireworks went off. I could smell the smoke from the bonfires. It always seemed to me that it was misty and slightly foggy if not raining on Guy Fawkes Night. I had never been to a Guy Fawkes party I imagined that they would be very enjoyable affairs.

I always enjoyed Bonfire Night in Ireland. My mind wandered back to my home town and Bonfire Night on our road to when the school bell rang and we tumbled out the school gate of the Salesian Convent, a Sister standing sentry duty at the gate. The joy of being set free from school was greeted by a beautiful spring afternoon. Meeting and greeting friends, our talk was on Bonfire Night.

It was a ritual set in ancient times. It was called the Festival of Light; all fires had to be put out on that day. The king lit the first fire to begin the celebrations for a good and fruitful harvest. St Patrick knew not to change old ways, so on 26th March 433AD, he lit the first fire before the king could light his and called it the Pascal Easter Vigil to celebrate the Light of Christ.

We were more interested in the preparations for the bonfire and if we thought about it the Festival of Light; it sounded good to us. We would celebrate for the ancestors both old and new and in return, we would be allowed to stay out late and enjoy the fun.

The collection of materials to burn on the night had already begun. It had to be a vast amount; the fire had to last well into the night. Mothers were constantly harassed with "can I have this for the bonfire?" It was a good time to clear out the sheds and back yards. The frenzy built up as we neared the day. Children, young and old on Farranshone, could be seen carrying bundles to Meaney's field.

The boys in charge organised the laying out of the bonfire and accepted or rejected the donations to the fire. Soon there was a giant bonfire ready and the time was appointed when the fire would be lit.

At the appointed hour we gathered in Meaney's field and the excitement escalated as the boys told us to stand well back. A torch was lit and with it several points around the fire burst into flame, cheers erupted. Suddenly the dark night sky lit up on that chilly, starry sky. We gazed in wonderment into the flames and felt a warm glow.

Mothers stood in small groups chatting, keeping a sharp lookout for children moving out of the light of the fire and being swallowed up in the darkness. What were you up to in the dark...? Children played games running in and out caught in the glowing light of the fire, laughing and calling out to one another. Groups of girls engrossed in deep conversation, whisperings of secret romance, latest films and music, Boys teased and taunted.

Boys put potatoes on the embers. I was handed one, it split and revealed a white flowery potato bursting out of its jacket, a knob of butter and I was in heaven.

We stood around listening to snippets of adult conversation as the Mammies gathered closer to the fire. The kind and ever generous Mrs Meaney, supplied cups of tea and music from her window ledge drifted over the field until the call for home and bed.

I had to put away carefree youthful memories. I lingered for a few moments longer before I went indoors, returned to my children and to bed. I longed for one moment, to escape, to live a little and have some fun.

There was a compulsory purchase order on the house in Connacht Road as the owner never did repairs. He just collected the rent money. The room we were in was a large room with kitchen. The kitchen in its former glory was a conservatory. It now held a cooker and the roof leaked. When I walked on the kitchen carpet it squelched under my feet. My son was four-and-a-half months old. He got an infection in his eye. I took him to the doctor and it cleared.

The man who owned the house came to collect the rent. John tried to reason with him and there was a lot of commotion. He said we had to get out. It did not matter that John knew him. I met the owner many times over the years. I thought about how he could do that to us. I never said a word about it to him as he did not appear to be better off himself. He had spent his money and had nothing to show for it.

Chapter 48

Getting A Mortgage

John told me to look for a house The distance from his work could not be more than half a crown return fare per day. I went off with that in mind and I saw a house. It was one shilling and three pence each way. John came with his cousin Elmo to view the house. They were happy, it was a good house. It was owned by a retired English couple and was in good condition. They were moving to the country. The house was nice and it had a garage, I would have willingly made a home in the garage. The owners agreed on a price.

I applied for a council loan, which would have been at a low interest rate. We had to wait four weeks, me phoning the council over the weeks, to see how they were progressing. I was told it went to committee, to be approved and I would know on the Friday, when the council would finish their meeting by lunch time. I had my lunch in the canteen and there was a phone in the cafeteria. I rang the council and the council employee said, "It did not go to the committee." I asked him why and he said "They had not received one document." I said, "You told me, it would go for approval. Where was the missing document?" He said, "In a room across the hall, from where the meeting was held." I broke down and cried.

When I had applied for a council mortgage, a lady from the council came to see our living conditions in Connacht Road. She said to me, "I cannot put you forward for re-housing, as you moved into the room after the council put the compulsory purchase order on the house." I informed her, "We are buying a house, we just need your report to help us get a council mortgage." The council lady did a report on the conditions of the house and our room, as a requirement for our council mortgage.

I left the office after the phone call with the council and went to the Abbey National Building Society. The manager was very nice to me. John had saved £1,100. The manager said it was a very good savings for a young couple. I was twenty-two and John was twenty-six. I did not mention that I had two children. I knew it would influence him. He asked if John could come in to sign the paperwork. I said he could not take a day off work. The manager gave me the paperwork to get him to sign. I brought the papers home and we both signed the mortgage papers. The next day I brought them back and asked for the manager. He came to the counter. There were a lot of people queuing up to pay their money into the building society, mostly West Indians. He quickly looked at the signatures.

When he saw our name, he said, "Where does your husband come from? We have a policy; you have to be so many years in this country before we lend you money." I was on a tightrope waiting for something else to appear, out of thin air and take the promise of a roof over our heads away. I slightly raised my voice and said, "My husband was in the Royal Engineers." I lied; we had been friends with two boys, one from Somerset and one a Londoner. They were also in the Royal Engineers. They fought for Queen and country. He surely would not refuse them. It was not my habit to lie but I was fighting for my family. I embarrassed the manager as people in the queue were listening. He said, "Oh, that is fine." He shuffled the papers a little embarrassed and we got the mortgage.

We went back to see the house as arranged and to let the owners know that the mortgage was through. The lady of the house said, "I am sorry but I will have to put up the price of the house. The owners have raised the price of the house I am buying. There is nothing I can do." It was called gazumping and was done a lot in the Sixties. I had worked out the budget and I did not have a penny over, after paying the solicitor, the deposit for the house and a deposit for the furniture. The mortgage was agreed and could not be changed. I explained all this to her to no avail. We went ahead with the purchase of the house. I then had to go to the bank and ask to borrow a hundred pounds. Again I had to lie and say my husband's cousin owed him a hundred pounds and agreed to pay him weekly. The manager knew we were buying the house and would not extend us a loan, if he thought we could not pay it back. I was convincing, we got the loan.

John and his cousin next moved us to a room owned by a Guyanese Indian family. A quiet little Indian girl would knock on my door and spend hours sitting on a chair watching me do work. I would say to her when John came home "I have to give John his dinner now." She would say, "That is OK" and still sit in his chair. I would then say, "You have to go now, he would not like it." I knew it would not bother him. I was in fear she would move in with us. It was coming up to Christmas and we were hoping to move to our new house and spend our first Christmas there. It was not to be. The solicitor slowed down with the exchange of paperwork in the weeks leading to Christmas.

On Christmas Eve, John went to visit his cousins to wish them happy Christmas. He stayed late. It was better in the Sixties to stay and sleep overnight at family or friends, if it got too late. It was well known that when men came out of the pub with drink taken, they could start a fight if they saw a West Indian or Indian man on their own on the street. John knew that he left me with the children at home so he was anxious to return. A policeman stopped him and asked him, "Where are you going to at this time of night?" He said "home" and kept walking. When he got to the bottom of the road a police car picked him up and brought him to Harlesden police station. They put him in a cell. He kept calling for the officer in charge. After some time he came and opened the cell door. He explained to the officer he was trying to get home to his family. The officer said, "Go and do not let it happen again." He was so relieved, he did not ask, 'do what?' again. He arrived after 4am. I had been dosing and waking all night, worried and waiting on his return.

Chapter 49

Exchange Contracts

5th January 1968 was the date the solicitor exchanged contracts on the house. Then we moved in the same day. It was a very cold day; it started to snow heavily with icy conditions everywhere. On 25th November we had ordered the furniture for the house, in the expectation of moving in before Christmas. As the furniture shop opened we were there at the door on a cold, empty street with the deposit of £40.7.6, the total cost of the furniture was £257.7.6. It furnished the entire house. I walked around the shop pointing to items: I will have one of that, one of that. We knew we would have to rent a flat in the house. We were not earning a lot and had to pay back the bank loan of one hundred pounds and the furniture. We first asked the manager of the furniture shop, could they deliver the day we moved and they agreed.

The shop was called Williams furniture in Harlesden. I wanted a three-piece suite. It cost £51.19.6 and could double up as a bed, in case we had visitors and I wanted a display cabinet £27.6.0 for my sitting room, a bedroom suite, a double and single bed, two sets of tables and chairs for the sitting rooms and two easy chairs for the upstairs sitting room.

We went to the house after picking up the keys from the solicitor and paying him his fee of £100. We moved our belongings which were not many into the house. The furniture had not arrived as yet. It was a cold empty house. Our heat was the paraffin fire and we lit the coal fire. The pipes were frozen. I turned on the bathroom sink tap to see if the water was running. The toilet would not flush as the pipes had frozen. Then John turned it off. I must have turned it on again. I was sitting on the carpet in the sitting room with the children as the house warmed, I heard the water come from the ceiling in the kitchen. The water could not go down the sink drain so it overflowed in the sink. I quickly sorted it and again sat on the carpet and looked around. There were little cracks on the plaster of the ceiling.

I started to cry. I thought, how did I not notice this, when I came to view the house. I thought it was a very serious matter. I was so busy looking around and taking in the room when I viewed the property that I forgot to check the ceilings. The furniture arrived and John started to assemble the beds. It was getting warmer. The kitchen was heaven to me. Everything was clean and shiny with the new furniture. I unpacked our belongings and made a home. The dining room was converted to our bedroom and the small bedroom for my daughter. My son had a cot in our room. The two bedrooms upstairs we made into a flat, the large bedroom a sitting room and the second room a back bedroom. Our sitting room was the front room downstairs.

The snow came down heavily; no vehicles could come down our cul-de-sac as the wind had blown the drift towards the end of the road. The house was cosy as we left the paraffin fire on all night in the hall downstairs. The heat rose and kept the house warm. When you lit the coal fire downstairs it heated the water, sometimes you could hear boiling water bubbling in the water pipes.

Before I went to sleep I looked into my spotless kitchen with great pleasure. I checked my daughter in her bedroom. The bathroom was dry with no sign of the earlier water disaster. I was not sure how I felt. Living out of a suitcase for so many years, you are constantly waiting for the next disaster. You build up a picture of what it is going to be like, when you have your own home. It is life, it comes with strings. Before I got the house I would go to sleep saying a poem in my head. It was called 'An Old Woman Of the Road' by Padraic Colum. It starts, 'O to have a little house.' Some people pray. I said the poem which was a form of prayer to me.

Chapter 50

Sharing Our Home

Within a few days of moving in, the post littered the hall. Bills, bills, bills, rates, water rates, connection fees, gas, electricity, telephone. The pressure started to show on John, who was not used to bills. He paid the rent and that was that. He started to quarrel about the light being left on all over the house. In the end I told him to leave what money he could on the table and to walk past all the mail when he came through the door and not open an envelope. For the rest of his life, he never opened an envelope that looked like a bill. If mail came for him from his family, I gave it to him. He took money from the bank account when he needed it. He was very reasonable with what he took; I never had to check what he took. If I said we could go on a holiday we would go, although it was some time before we went on our first family holiday together. If I did not mention it to him, he knew we could not afford it.

News got around that we'd bought a house and we had a visit on a very cold night from Dean. We knew Dean from the community we were in. As the years went by he became a lifelong friend. He wanted to ask us if we could rent a flat to June and Robin. June was related to him, she had two girls the eldest was Joan and the baby Ester. Joan was around my daughter's age and Ester was just born. They were desperate for a flat and I knew how it felt. I had seen them several times but not spoken to them. We agreed they could have the flat upstairs and share the bathroom and kitchen. They moved in two weeks later.

June resembled the beggar maid in the painting of *King Cophetua and the Beggar Maid* in an 1884 painting by the Pre-Raphaelite artist Edward Burne-Jones. June was tall and slim with delicate features resembling the face of the beggar maid in the painting. She carried herself with pride, spoke gently and quietly. She was a pleasant and well-mannered lady. They were both of

Indian descent. I got on very well with June. There was something strange about Robin. I had to be constantly on the alert when he came downstairs to use the kitchen. If the kitchen door was closed he would always open the door under the stairs and stand there. I would go to the hall, say "not that door" and show him the kitchen door. Robin was from Grenada and had been a teacher. He was handsome, well built, without being fat. He dressed well. It was known that he had been a school teacher, his reserve was respected and it had been read as part of his personality. His quiet demeanour meant that he had good standing in the community, this very reserve masked the fact that he suffered from the early onslaught of Alzheimer's disease, little was known of this condition in the Sixties. I did not ask him questions or engage him in conversation. He would help June when she instructed him to do a task. If I saw him standing, looking lost in the kitchen, not quite knowing what to do next I would judge what he was meant to do and help him.

Joan and Louise, my daughter, became good friends and play mates. Ester was a sweet child with a winning smile. She was two weeks when she came to live with us so I saw her grow. When the older children played in the back garden they would come to the kitchen window while I was cooking. Joan would say Louise is doing, saying this and then Louise would come saying Joan is saying, doing this. I would sympathise with both. They would run off happily to resume their play.

The two girls started school on the same day; they looked so lovely in their school uniforms. We took photographs in the back garden to mark their first day. Louise was so petite; I had to turn up all her clothes. Her navy coat had such a large turn up, I was sure it would last her for the first three to four years of her school life. It was the smallest size they had.

One day I heard an explosion in the kitchen. When I went to investigate Robin had put a tin of baby food to boil and forgotten it. It was spread all over the kitchen ceiling and walls. He had forgotten it was on the boil, the water evaporated and it blew up.

It was time to speak to June. She told a dark story. "Robin had a girlfriend, he'd left her, the girl's mother was involved in the black arts." She went on, "I was told that Robin's girl friend's mother gave him some food to eat and had sprinkled a powder on the food and that was why he could not remember anything." This explanation for severe illness is easier to accept than the reality. If one could get something to reverse the illness, the person would be back to normal. People have been known to pay vast sums of money, to people who deal in black magic, to get a cure. When they say they can cure a sick person, saying. "Someone did him something" but not specifying what that something was. Saying "they put something in his food" was a common saying at that time. It would account for a severe unexplained illness in the West Indies. It was easier to accept as an explanation. When you looked at a strong healthy man, who could not remember or think for himself it was hard to understand. I talked to her for a long time persuading her to see the logic of what she was saying; that this could not happen, she should take him to the doctor. She said, "Marie, it will make no difference." Every time he had an episode we had discussions, she felt better after our discussions and I was left feeling distressed and depressed.

I was working at Glacier Metal at the time; it was five minutes from my home. I could come home at lunchtime and see my son and feed him, hoover the carpet or put a wash on. June was looking after him. Robin was also working at Glacier Metal, he got progressively worse, they gave him menial tasks to do such as cleaning the yard and sweeping up. I overheard a woman saying, "He is creepy, he just stands there lost."

At this time June had a miscarriage. She was in a hospital some distance from where we lived. I had to take Robin and the four children with me to see her. The two younger ones were little. It was very difficult making sure that Robin stayed with us. On the way back travelling home, changing buses was a nightmare with four children: Getting Ester and my son out of the pushchair; carrying Ester in one arm while loading the pushchair on the bus with the other hand and then getting my son by the hand and boarding the bus. I was aware people were looking at me struggling and Robin strong and healthy, standing there and not helping.

When we changed the bus, we could not all sit together we were at the front and Robin was at the back. I paid for us all. I told the bus conductor I was paying for Robin. The bus was crowded, when the conductor got to Robin and asked him for his fare, Robin did not understand him and kept looking at him. The conductor thought he was trying to avoid paying. He started shouting, "You people are all the same, always trying to avoid paying your fare." I had to shout to be heard over the heads of standing passengers. I said, "I have paid his fare. I have his ticket." The next stop Robin got off which was a stop before our stop. He was upset, he knew something was not right, he did not understand what, he saw the cross look on the conductor's face. He just could not do anything about it. I had to walk back from our stop with the pushchair and the four children to make sure he got home safely.

Chapter 51

Dean's Story

Dean came to England around the time John came, the difference was that Dean left his wife and children to come to the UK and make a better life for them. He was already in his thirties. Who can understand the thinking of another human being or what made him take that decision? John and Dean were like brothers and I looked to him as a brother-in-law. I have to be fair and say many families felt they owned a piece of Dean and that he belonged to them. It was a way he distanced himself from close contact. Friends with all, close, but not too close with any. When you are an immigrant you build your own community and your new family within it.

There was a disadvantage for Dean as he was alone, with one pay packet. The money left after he paid for the rent of his room, food and travel to work, was very little. He did not have a well-paying job. He would send what he could, it was never enough. There was none left to save.

His wife's sisters were very good to his children, they were a united family, the aunts were teachers and they encouraged his children to studies. It is hard to say they would not have done as well in England. I believe they were studious and would have done well anywhere, as was proved later in their lives. I remember him going to Foyle's Book Store in London to get accounting books to send for his son, who was studying accountancy. His children in later life were very successful in many countries, outside of Trinidad and in Trinidad. He would not have been able to furnish them with a house in England. They had one in Trinidad and a large extended family. He saw the misery of emigrants living in rooms, with low incomes and low expectations. One could say why did he not go home? He had a job in Trinidad before he left.

He was artistic, he sometimes painted in oils, as a hobby. He had talent but did not believe in himself. He would destroy his painting when he finished, as it did not look as he thought it should. He never had training in art and he could not afford art classes. The same was true about his voice. He could sing very well and with training he could have been good, but never learned his songs. When he first came to England he went to have voice training but the cost was prohibitive. Failure is very hard for proud people. Had he returned to Trinidad he would have been the man who did not make it.

The money he sent was never enough but it was all he had. When he lived at home, he handed over his pay packet. When he sent money home, he had to save every cent and start again. He did the best he could do and though he was not there for his children in person, he talked about them with pride and their successes in education were his joy.

I never saw him get close to another woman. He has passed over now. When he lived, he was loved and respected by everyone he met. He is still talked about with affection. He did not spend his time in pubs drinking. If you asked him to dinner, he might or might not come. Friends would say you know what he is like.

I believe he had a fear of getting close to anyone, a private person when it came to his family; people have a tendency to ask questions about one's private life. We all wanted him to join our company as he lightened our lives with his stories of Trinidadian life. He made us laugh. I will never understand why a man who leaves his family is treated like a deserter but a man who leaves, divorces and marries again can be loved and respected by his old and new family.

June had a cousin Alice and her friend Ruth. They were both nurses. Alice was a theatre nurse and Ruth was a midwife. They worked long hours and very hard. Sometimes on their day off they would visit June and Robin and it was a happy time for me also. They knew about Robin's condition. They could do nothing to help him. Their visits were enjoyed by all.

The kitchen would get very lively and busy as they liked to cook home food. They would chat and laugh as they busied themselves. In the hospital where the nurses worked, because of their unsocial hours, they ate mostly in the canteen, so when the opportunity arose to visit, they would cook Roti, curry, bake a cake and make sweets. We would eat together; there would be talk about family and friends in Trinidad. I had a picture in my mind of their families. I got to know their family and friends through their conversations long before I went to Trinidad and met them.

On the occasion when Alice went home on holiday, her family cooked and froze food. Before she left they brought it wrapped in tin foil, well packed in a hand luggage bag, to give her as she was leaving on the plane for England. That would not be allowed by customs today. When she arrived, that afternoon they prepared the food so that John and June's cousin, Dean, would join the party when they came from work. We feasted on King Prawns cooked in a dry curry, curried duck, dal pori, curried mano. She would bring pepper and mango chutney, sweet breads, black cake, a bottle of Trinidad rum and the latest Caribbean music.

When Alice rested we all got together. There was always the tape of the latest music released for the carnival, an LP brought as a gift for John and a Safari shirt from Alice's brother Simon, a crochet or lace tray cloth sent for me, handmade by Alice's mother who was a gifted needle worker, as are a lot of the older Caribbean women. She made me a tablecloth of linen with a pattern of pulled stitches which looked like lace work.

We would play the record that was gifted to us over and over again, never getting tired of it. The food would be prepared, rum and Coca Cola with ice and lemon all round. We listened to the latest Indian or calypso music playing on the turntable.

We would all hear about Trinidad, The latest Election, which party was in power, what they were not doing for Trinidad. As we sat around the table we listened to the stories of Alice's holiday in awed silence, her picnics in the hills, by the river, fresh fish broth made with King Fish, bought on the creek, straight from the sea, hours before they travelled to the hills for a picnic.

The men cooked the fish broth in a big iron pot, over an open fire. It was the men's pleasure to cook outdoors, barbecue or any other dish. They all joined in and excelled in their cooking, as it was part of the activities of the day. The men would also cook for and serve at weddings and leave the ladies to enjoy the day.

The supplies for the fish broth were brought by the ladies of the party together with Roti and curried duck cooked from home.

They would swim in the fresh cool water of the hill and enjoy the company of friends and family, food and drink. She also went with family to parties on the beach and swam in the warm waters of the Caribbean Sea.

The talk around the table never slowed as a question would be thrown in from time to time. What about Mr so and so, questions about aunty and uncle. Our minds travelled to the island and we relived every moment with Alice. It was such a lovely time and holds great memories. Alice's sister in Trinidad was a very fine cook and the combination of flavours of West Indian spices. Trinidad rum, music and good company was a recipe for success.

Chapter 52

Agency Work

I went to work with the agency at Sumlock comptometer school, at Hanger Lane. It was hard to maintain a job, when a babyminder without warning, would tell you that she had an appointment the next day and could not mind your baby. I felt very guilty about letting down my employer, guilty if my child was sick and I had to leave the baby at the nannies. I felt less stress when I joined the agency. I worked for them at many companies; I lost count of the number. I could say to the agency, "I cannot come to work this week." They would replace me at the company I was working at, on their behalf...

My younger sister had come over to work in the UK. She got a room on our road with a neighbour and worked locally. One evening she was in the kitchen while I was cooking. I had been sick. John came in and sensed all was not well. My sister said, "Marie is sick." He looked at me and I said, "I am pregnant." He was very cross and said, "You know we cannot afford it." That was his worry until I gave birth. I now see when he looked at the members living in our household. It looked as if we were responsible for them all.

When my time came near, I asked Sumlock comptometers agency, if I could work from home. I would walk up to Hanger Lane with the children, collect the work and give them back the finished work, which was mainly stock sheets and payroll calculations. I would visit the small library at Hanger Lane on my way back and then come home. This work gave me enough income to manage.

Robin was getting no better. When he forgot what he was doing, June would send Joan his daughter to remind him. When she could not get through to him she would get frustrated. She would be upset and sound cross. He did not understand but knew it was not right for a small child to be disrespectful to a parent. I would come out of my room and smooth the troubled waters. I could not explain to Joan that he was ill. I could not put a name to it. She once said to me, "I have never known my Daddy to be well."

June, Robin and the children would go to church on Saturday. When you saw Robin dressed smartly and the family looking good, you would not guess Robin's illness or June's anguish. He looked strong and healthy. June still had not brought him to the doctor. Her belief of the damage the Black Arts could do, was deeply set in her brain, or maybe she did not want to face up to the reality of his illness. She had heard of some potent that could turn a human being into a zombie. She strongly believed this was the case. I spent many hours reassuring her, again feeling her distress. We lived more like family than landlord and tenant. Robin's illness was a family illness. Dean, June's family member, periodically visited and lightened our life with stories of what was happening in the community and stories of Trinidadian life.

Chapter 53

Birth Of Mia

We always believe that our babies are babies until they do something that shows they have their own thoughts. We were at a wedding of a family member. Louise was a flower girl. She looked very pretty with her long beautiful hair dressed in her white satin dress with a purple sash. I was standing at the side, holding my son's hand and watching. I was heavily pregnant at the time with my youngest daughter, Mia.

My son was just over two. To me he was my baby. The photographer was calling for groups to be photographed. He called for the groom and his best man and male cousins. They were all lined up when my son pulled away from my hand and joined the group dead centre. He stood up in front of the group, to have his photograph taken. I stood in amazement. He'd found his place on the planet. He was a male and his place was with the male members of the family, not on the sidelines holding his Mammy's hand. It is always an awaking moment, when your babies think for themselves and shows an independence of spirit in action. It comes as a shock to see them grow up with confidence and know their place in society.

On 16th November 1969 I went into hospital to give birth to a lovely baby girl named Mia. One of the nurses kept saying "Call her Tracy, she looks like a Tracy." I thought, no that is not her name. I had a lovely midwife and she lived locally, I would meet her often in the next two years. When John came to see his daughter the next morning, she was in the nursery. He went in to see her, on his way to see me and said, "I knew she was my daughter, all my children have the same shaped head of hair." He was delighted with Mia. She was a beautiful child with dark eyes and dark hair and a winning smile.

The next day I had a visit from June. She was looking after my son Allen while I was in hospital. She started telling me that she left her daughter Ester aged two years and my son, two years and six months, while she went out on the road to buy meat from the butcher's. She said, "I had to leave Allen and Ester for a little while and go to the butcher's. It did not take long. I rushed all the way, on my return. As I put the key in the front door I could smell smoke. I ran up the stairs. The room was filled with black smoke; the children were huddled together in the easy chair. I got hold of them in both arms and ran down the stairs and out of the house to the garden. I sat them on the grass and told them not to move. I went back inside the house to put the fire out. They had put three and a half inch vinyl records on the paraffin fire, they melted and caught fire. Do not worry the children are fine. There are some burns on the carpet and on the back of the chair. The insurance man came to collect his money and I told him about the fire. He will talk to you when you come out of hospital."

She had a paraffin fire, a tall cylinder type and the children were playing. They put some three and a half inch Vinyl records on top of the cylinder. She explained that the two children were huddled together sitting in one of the easy chairs. When they saw the smoke they must have been scared and sat on the chair together for comfort. I did not say a word. I just sat propped up against my pillows and looked at her in silence. I came out of the hospital a few days later.

My sister Phillis came to visit with her two children, my niece Ann and nephew Paul. They came to see me and the baby. Louise, Joan, Paul and Anna, played happily in the garden. Louise was always happy when her cousins came to visit.

June joined us in my living room to see baby Mia. She started to relate the story of the fire again, going into every detail. I got hysterical, sobbing my heart out. My sister said, "Drink a Guinness. It is good for your nerves when you have a baby; it is like an iron tonic." All I could see was the two little ones together in the easy chair. My mind was going over and over, asking the question 'What if she did not come home on time? That is how they would be found, dead". "I still have flash backs, of the two little ones on the chair.

My son Allen was crying and I had to ask my husband to put him to bed. I have always regretted not giving him time that day, as he would have missed me. I should have put him to bed. Mia was fine she did not know any different.

John had been planning to go on holiday to Trinidad and I had booked his passage. It was ten years since he had left home. He was to leave about six weeks after the birth of our Mia. True to form, I did not allow time, for me going three weeks over my due date. John said he would cancel the holiday but I insisted no. He had not been home to see his family since he came to the UK. He and his family were looking forward to his return. He left as a young man and was returning as a family man with three children. He told me when he came out of the airport that his family did not recognise him. His brother- in-law came up to him and asked him if he was John. I was quiet happy to be on my own with the children at this time. I hoped to get some rest while he was away. I looked after a little girl who lived on our street while her Mom worked and looked after two children, after school until their Mom picked them up. I continued to take work from the agency.

Chapter 54

Mia's Christening

My daughter Mia was christened in St Joseph's Church in Wembley. There was a full house. I was up early as I had a lot to do beforehand. I was busy cooking for the after party. I had fed my children, given them their baths, dressed them. Then I gave my full attention to Mia. I gave Mia her bath and put on her christening gown. She looked like a little angel in her cot. I went into the kitchen to see how everything was progressing. I was preparing for a party, a lot of John's family and friends were expected after the christening.

I had asked my younger sister to be Mia's godmother. My husband and my sister came into the kitchen. They were fully dressed and ready to go. I was finishing the final preparations on the food for when everyone came. It may have been getting a little late nearing the time to leave for the church. John said, "We will take the baby to be christened, you stay and finish the food, you have a lot to do here. People will be coming to the house, you can let them in." I was devastated. The decision seemed to have been made and off they went. It all happened so quickly. When they came back my sister related in detail, a description of the christening not wanting me to miss anything. I am now told by her I was very upset. I had blocked it somehow from my mind to help me move on.

I have had many years to look back on the lack of decisiveness on my part. Why did I allow people to do this to me? Why did I not say 'No, you will not go without me I am Mia's mother'?" It was my baby's christening. I was overwhelmed. It takes time for me to react to a situation, it takes time for it to sink in, it takes time to absorb the facts when I am not expecting them; I have no warning that it is going to happen. They were gone so quickly, I blame myself. When they came back to the house it was filled with people. I could not say anything to John, as I was feeling very low. John would have said "I just thought you had too much to do, it was better this way." I just said nothing. I was never one to make a fuss and say no when faced with a decision that was already made.

I look at young people today and think they would not let that happen, they are decisive. They have the confidence to voice their opinions, say what they want and make a stand.

Chapter 55

Elmo's Story

Elmo floated in and out of our lives over the years. He had a special part in John's heart as it was his father who left the bequest to John's mother and her sisters. It was never mentioned and I did not know if he knew or not. He would not be refused a meal and a bed for the night in our house.

He was a man with a big personality. He carried himself well, like a man of wealth and importance. When he had a glass of red wine or two, which he was partial to, he was a great story teller. I'd known him for many years. On a wet afternoon when John was at work, after the birth of my daughter, he told me stories of John's family. I got to know them through his recounting events that happened in the past. He had a good sense of humour and a voice that carried.

He was the bane of his family's life. His father came back to Grenada, on his first visit, after many years in the States and bought an estate for his eldest son, buses to run as a business for another and a fishing boat for Elmo. He told them if they doubled their money he would give them money again.

Both of the older boys did well. Elmo on the other hand did a little fishing, had a great time, sold the boat and drank the proceeds. He was not a lone drinker; he loved company and usually had an entourage when he had money. His mother who was a stern woman and never spoken of with affection, would ask, "Elmo, how's the boat going?" She knew everything that happened on the small island that concerned her and her family. He would say, "It is going good, Ma." She knew and he knew that the boat was sold. This was not a lie as it was going good, in another person's hands.

He'd had a brother who he was very fond of who died suddenly. Elmo drowned his sorrow in drink for a few days and would not go to the funeral. He told me, that on the night of the funeral after all who attended had left the graveyard; he went to his brother's grave, lay beside it and slept all night.

His father returned again after many years and was happy with the two older boys' progress. Elmo went on a binge drinking and kept away, not wanting to face him, but after a few days his father sent for him. He did not say how he was received. I am sure he had a good cover story. I think his father was very fond of the black sheep of the family.

His brothers were embarrassed with his behaviour and his drinking. One day they got him drunk and talked him into going to England. With his mother's permission, they put him on a ship to England. They gave money to the purser, with instructions to give the money to him, just before he landed in England and was due to leave the ship. He persuaded the purser to give him his money immediately he boarded the ship.

It was the custom for ladies travelling to the UK to bring a bottle of white rum for their family. A glass of white rum would be given if you had a fever on a winter's day or to soak fruits for a black cake for Christmas. He told them to sell it to him, on the grounds that the law had changed in England and they could no longer bring alcohol into the UK.

He arrived at our house excitable and very decisive on one occasion, as he got news, that his mother had died and he was going home to claim his inheritance. He arrived with an entourage, settled into our sitting room, borrowed money from John and had a wake for his mother. On the second day of his stay news arrived, through a cousin phoning home to ask what were the funeral arrangements, only to be told that Elmo's mother had not died. She was alive and kicking. He made a quick exit with his friends. Life went back to normal and we did not see him for a number of months.

On one occasion, he stayed overnight and slept on the couch in our sitting room. I had a collection of miniature bottles of wine, brandy and whisky on display in my glass cabinet. I was very proud of. I collected them when I travelled or they were given to me. In the morning I went to clean the front room and found Elmo had drunk the lot. He said not to worry, he would replace them. There was no point in worrying, as I knew they would never be replaced. I realised it was not a good idea to have any alcohol in the house as the temptation for him was too great.

He arrived on one occasion and I knew he was ill. He slept on the couch that converted into a bed in the sitting room. I was very worried as I thought he would be dead when I came in from work or my daughter from school. I asked John to talk to him and tell him to go and see the doctor as the doctor's surgery was very near our house. They called an ambulance and sent him to hospital, he had an enlarged heart and fluid had to be extracted. He did not drink alcohol after that. In the past he occasionally had dry spells, lasting months but he would return to drink in the end.

Some months later, on a Saturday morning, in a cousin's house, he was sitting with a group of his cousins and John, watching a horse race on television. I forgot to mention betting on the horses was a sport he enjoyed and partook of, in a great way. He studied the form, the trainers, the weight the horse carried and the quality of the turf: soft, hard, wet or dry and the past wins of the horses. Sometimes he won, never a million.

This takes me back to my childhood and the day of the Grand National which prompted a re-enactment of the race on our road.

The horse ESB seemed to be the favourite at 20 to1.

Eamon, one of my neighbours, was very knowledgeable about the race and after much discussion a decision was made, we would have our own Grand National in Meaney's field. The word went out that we were going to have an enactment of the race. We arrived at Meaney's field the next day, Dermot, Eamon and I. Children from the road drifted towards the field in one's and two's and small groups.

It was a very serious affair everyone was involved with the building and layout of the fences, the track spread around the whole field. All matters were handled in a very businesslike way. Eamon was the expert, Dermot an organiser and I would like to think, I was the Steward.

Becher's Brook was discussed in detail and a pit dug to represent the water. The fences were scaled down to accommodate the needs of our smaller jockeys. There may not have been as many as 16 fences, the important ones were there, to us it was perfection.

Children were dispersed in all directions to build the fences with sticks, branches, logs and anything that they could get their hands on. Instructions were given and when all were satisfied, that the fences were as near as possible to the Grand National ones. The jockeys gathered at the starting line, while their horses, as figments of their imagination, were kept in order. They pounced around dancing and jumping at the starting line, pulling on the imaginary leads as if they were trying to control a high spirited horse. The starter pistol went off and there were one or two false starts.

At last we had a good start, around the course; with great speed they jumped the fences. Some jumping, some ran around Becher's Brook. They raced with wild abandonment, legs flaying in the air, jostling for position. They finished with the water jump, which was more a long jump than a high jump.

The scene was a mixture of shouts of excitement, colour and faces strained with consecration. Younger children cheered as spectators. A few smiling mothers, arms folded, viewed the scène.

The cows in the next field took little notice and continued to chew the cud.

Eamon was master of ceremonies, accordingly elevated on a high seat with great dignity. I do not think there were any prizes, Congratulations and to be acknowledged as a winner, was enough. A great day was had by all. We went home to our tea, happy in the knowledge that we had a great day at the races.

At John's cousin's house, John looked over at Elmo and saw his cigarette was burning a hole in his trouser leg. He had a bet on a horse called Night Nurse and it won. He passed away while watching the race; the excitement was too much for his weak heart. I cried a lot at his funeral. He was the only family that I had grown close to since I married John. He was an uncle, I was fond of. I now wonder, if it was a sense of loss, or relief that I could now have a wine cellar, if I wanted to, or could afford it. It was the first death I experienced in England; it brought back to mind another time and the death of my uncle.

Uncle Dominic, Daddy's older brother was a tall heavy man. My father would say, "In his youth he could dance the hornpipe (an Irish dance) on the table, even though he was a big lad, he was that light on his feet." He came to visit our house in Limerick, after a family funeral one night with Daddy. When they had supper, he sat in the armchair by the fire. He took out a small box with cloves of garlic and chewed them. He offered one to me, but I declined. Even then he must have known that he was in poor health. Heads of garlic are good for cardiovascular disease. You can reduce cholesterol by ingesting garlic and I am told it is good for the plaque deposits on the walls of your veins.

My Mammy and I went over to Uncle Dominic's house the moment that Daddy gave us the news that his brother had passed away. My Aunt Ita, his sister, was in hospital seriously ill with cancer and Uncle Dominic was at home getting ready to go and visit her. He went to the hospital to see her every day. The hospital was very near his house. It was the month of fasting for Lent. He liked a drink but decided to give it up for Lent. Aunt Ita was his second mother after his mammy died. He was feeling a great deal of stress, as was all the family. His teenage son Paddy was with him getting a clean shirt for him and polishing his shoes, when he collapsed and died.

We arrived at the house soon after we heard the news. Aunty Lena was sitting by the fire with friends and close neighbours repeating over and over again, "He was in the kitchen with Paddy, he was having a shave before going to visit his sister Ita in hospital. I heard a crash and Paddy calling for me, he was on the floor, one look and I knew he was gone." She seemed to derive some comfort from going through the motions of repeating every detail of his last movements to every newcomer who entered her house.

My cousin Mary Kate said, "Come with me, I do not want to go to his room alone." We went up the stairs together. We entered the room where a nurse was putting the finishing touches to laying him out. I stood in the door, afraid to enter the room. My cousin was a grown up, a pretty girl with red hair and much older than me. She opened the window and covered the mirror, turning the pictures towards the wall. I said, "Mary Kate, why are you covering the mirror?" She told me, "You open the window to allow the spirit to leave the room." One of the superstitions is that the next person to see themselves in the mirror will be the next person to die. "The mirror is covered to allow the spirit to pass to the next life successfully, if Daddy saw his soul in the mirror he would get trapped in this life," she said. "After the funeral we can remove the cover from the mirror and put everything back to normal."

I said a prayer as a neighbour started the Rosary and visitors came up the narrow stairs to pay their respects and say a prayer. I was glad to make my escape down the stairs where there was tea, lemonade, whiskey for the men, sherry for ladies and cake on offer. I took my lemonade and cake and went to the kitchen leaving the adults to relate stories about the deceased. Uncle Dominic's son Paddy was in the kitchen. He was older than me: a quiet, shy boy. We just stood together by the window not saying much. He started to draw cartoons for me I was very impressed as he was very good. It started to get late and Mammy was ready to go home.

She and I walked past King John's Castle over the bridge and home, it was dark and I was tired. Mammy talked, I tucked my hand in her arm. I do not remember too much of what she said, I was not required to answer. I was tired and dazed with a lot to think about, after the day's happenings.

Weeks later I was in town with Mammy and we met Mary Kate, Uncle Dominic's daughter. Mammy asked her how they were coping. She said, "Paddy had a nervous breakdown. He was very close to his Dad, he could not eat anything as he would bring it up again. He had to go into hospital for depression. The doctors were very worried about his condition. We were told that it was a bad time for him to suffer depression, during his adolescent years." He recovered and later married but my memory of him remained as a slightly withdrawn, quiet, young man.

A wake is the night vigil, praying and watching over the deceased from time of death to burial it is an important part of the grieving process in many cultures and we now saw cousin Elmo off in style.

Chapter 56

The Diamond Ring

Money was always scarce. I did a budget every January, it was the longest month of the year. I would base it on last year's bills, pocket money, travel money and clothes. When you have spent all your money to make the Christmas a success, it is a very long month. I would then do, a "to- get" list: a new carpet for one of the bedrooms, a bathroom set and new net curtains. At the time, I did the budget and a "to-get" list I had very little hope of getting all the things as there was no spare money. At the end of the year I would be very amazed that I bought all that was on last year's list. It is surprising to see that the cost was not enormous. I managed the money well and we paid our bills.

I had never had an engagement ring. I got one after I was married one Christmas. The diamond was so small and the ring so thin, I nearly asked, did it come with a magnifying glass, so I could see if there really was a diamond. I did not, as I did not want to seem ungrateful.

Years later John got a private job painting some vehicles, which was a very rare occurrence. He worked very hard over some weekends. Then one Saturday, he came home at 2pm had a shower and said to me, get the children ready, we are going to get you a ring. We all went off in high spirits, me not quiet believing my luck. We had three children by then.

It was a time of recession, there was a general slowdown in the economy, several high street shops closed down. We were passing a jewellery shop. There was a large notice in the window "Closing down sale".

The shop was full. One of the jewellers came up to us. John said, "She wants an engagement ring." I do not remember asking for a ring.

The jeweller scanned our little group three young children, one a baby in arms. He took in our little group in one quick glance and asked how much John wanted to spend.

He then measured my finger; he went to the display window and picked a ring. It was beautiful. I am sure the good man gave us a very good deal.

Young people now would not find that it was bling enough, or impressive enough, or a large enough diamond. I knew the work that John did, to earn the money to pay for it and the diamond ring was perfect and brilliant for me.

Chapter 57

Education At 24 Years

I came to England when I was seventeen.. I left school before doing my intermediate certificate. I had three children by the time I was twenty-four, a house and a mortgage.

What motivated me was my Dad. He said to me, "An educated man is an educated individual and an educated woman is an educated family." He was fond of quotes in key places. This quote he got from an African proverb. He realised the benefits of education and the importance of a woman's education in the family. He was trying to get me interested in school at the time. It did not work. I wanted my life to start. When I had children, I realised the mother spends more time with the children therefore, they have more influence. When I stopped work for maternity leave, it was two months before and six weeks after the birth of my baby. I was paid maternity leave by the National Insurance, for fourteen weeks and when it finished I went back to work.

I decided to educate myself, so I took myself off to the library together with my two children. While walking to Hanger Lane, where there was a small library, I decided to check on the science books. At school we were not taught sciences, we did domestic economy. Boys' schools did science. Girls were expected to get married, stop work and have a family in that order. I settled my daughter with books, my son was two.

I did not know where to start. The only person I thought of, as a scientist was Charles Darwin; I collected a book or two on Evolution. I read, devouring every word. Darwin's travels, through the Galapagos Islands, the voyage of the Beagle and the *Origin of Species*. His description of variation in plants and animals, as he moved through the islands, how they altered to accommodate finding food and adapting to their environment, in order to survive. This started me along a train of thought about man's creation. I was morose and distressed trying to accommodate my religious beliefs and Darwin's *Theory of Evolution*.

The trouble with leaving home young, you have normal development that happens in you earlier years. Corinthians 13:11 "when I was a child I spoke as a child, I understood as a child, I thought as a child: but now I am a man, I put away childish things."

You do not have grown-up values; you have not advanced mentally as yet. I have seen this with emigrants from all over the world. They have a tendency to cling to each other for support, not making friends outside their family or social groups. It takes about five years before they stick their heads up and look around. All religious and cultural values and beliefs that they came with, in their early development, stay with them. Some never change, others move on, when they are able to come to terms with their new surroundings.

On one of my trips I was pushing my son up to the library, waddling like a duck. I am 5ft 2ins and was carrying a lot of weight. I thought the trouble with my thought process is, I am not educated enough to make a decision on evolution. The words of a Negro spiritual came to mind, "The things in the Bible are not necessarily so" so I decided to leave the question of evolution until I got more knowledgeable. Years later I can accept the two living side by side. Seven days to make the world could be seven trillion, trillion years. As they say time is relative in space, it sounds good to me.

My next step was to read the European Classics. I was into books in a big way, a form of escapism from the harsh realities of life. I had read all the English classics, Jane Austen, Charles Dickens, Shakespeare's Sonnets, they were all my favourite books; I then started to read all the Russian writers.

While out with one of my friends, before I left home, I thought I would have an intellectual discussion. As we wandered along the high road, I asked her if she knew anything about the Iron Curtain. It was widely talked about, newspapers etc . . . My friend said, "You should not talk about that, my father said, 'It is very bad, do not go there'." I did not pursue the subject with her. So when I got the opportunity, I thought I should read Russian literature so that I would find out, what the people were like. Did they have two heads? I was happy to report they were normal, like any citizen of the world. I read over many years.

I discovered early what made a classic. When you read a sentence and it is familiar, you say, how true, I knew someone like that, it is in our everyday lives, you recognise it, but you did not, or could not have written it. Fyodor Dostoyevsky is said to have watched people's faces and mannerisms closely and used the knowledge to describe people in his books. He suffered from epilepsy; he portrayed this in one or more of his books. It was brought on when triggered by emotional distress again using experiences to write a classic. He was a spiritual and deeply religious person. He wrote, *The Brothers Karamazov*, but *The Idiot* was my favourite. Leo Tolstoy wrote *War and Peace* and many other books. I read the first volume when I was on holiday, with my family in Brighton, my husband walked on the promenade with the children and I read.

Turgenev's *First Love*, I liked very much. I read Honore de Balzac who wrote *Father Goriot*, a moving tale about his daughter's greed. I could not tell you all the books I read over the years, or the stories between the covers. I have lived many lives as a fly on the page of my books and have been very sad to come to the end of many.

I was not driven by ambition but by need. It was necessary to earn more money when you had children, to survive, to pay for child minders and educate your children. I could not wait on cost of living rises to survive. One could get a little more pay if you went agency or studied and got a better position, which is what I did. I studied.

While working for Sumlock Comptometers I saw their maintenance department taking apart the Sumlock machines, which came back for repair. I asked why. I was told that the new Anita Electronic Calculators would replace the Sumlock Comptometer. When the repairmen went to a company to repair the comptometer machine, they would take it away for repair, saying they needed a part for it. They would say they could not repair it. A salesman would introduce them to the calculator and proclaim its benefits. That it could easily be used, without much training. He was right of course, The Anita Calculators were too large at first but the manufacturer scaled them down. In 1973 Norman Rockwell of Rockwell Digital bought over Anita, Bell and Sumlock. That was the end of comptometers.

I decided to go to night school. I did English literature and language and RSA booking and principles of accounts in one year. The next year I signed up for business studies. Then I went on to do CIMA (Chartered Institute of Management Accountants). I did not complete the final year, another story for another time. I quickly realised that there would be a forced change in my career. Change was all around, I dreamed of sitting at a desk with a machine built in where I would do my calculations. That would have been the computer.

From the beginning, I worked on computerised accounts. I never did manual accounts. Keeping a set of books... I did business studies while working for the agency, one of my agency jobs was with Central Middlesex Hospital Management Committee. I worked for the treasurer doing manual spreadsheets, with hospital statistics, comparing our hospital figures to other hospitals with the same number of hospital beds. I would do depth audit, to see why ours was so much higher in certain areas. It was very interesting work, as I unravelled the reasons why our hospital costs were so high. The treasurer asked me to work as his technical assistant, I accepted. I continued working and studying.

I was assistant financial accountant at a company for twelve years and cost accountant for two years at another company. They closed. Then I moved to a job as company accountant for eighteen-and-a-half years. I retired from this company.

Chapter 58

Bad Start At School

L
ouise and Joan were at a school in Alperton and my son Allen and Mia were at a school in Perivale. Mia was in the nursery school and Allen was in first year infants. After dropping the younger ones off at school, I would walk from Perivale to Hanger Lane where the Sumlock Agency was. If I had a new company to go to, I would get the assignment and travel from there. Otherwise I would work at the agency.

Mothers and their children were all heading in the direction of the school. I was approached by a mother and her robust son, on my way back, after dropping my children to school. The lady told me that Allen attacked her son in class and scratched him on the hand. She lifted his hand, to show me a small scratch, she had been to see the headmaster.

Alarm bells started to ring. My son had not been eating well at dinner time, he was picking at his food. I put this down to him not being hungry. The school supplied a dinner at lunchtime and milk in the morning. He had also wet the bed which he never did before, it was not like him. I told the mother I knew nothing about this and I would go straight back to see the headmaster. I went to his office and said to him, "I believe there was a problem involving my son. What was the trouble? A lady told me my son was fighting in class. The headmaster said, "I am very annoyed with that lady, as I punished him in front of her. The woman should not have mentioned it to you. I caned him, it was done legally." He proceeded to show me where he had entered it in a punishment book. He said, "He was a brave little lad, he never cried." I turned and left the room, tears welling up in my eyes. I do not know if I said goodbye.

I went straight into action mode. I went to a Catholic school in Wembley and spoke to the headmistress who was a nun. I believed that a Catholic school would send for me, let me know what was happening and certainly not cane a child in front of a mother seeking vengeance. After I explained to her what had transpired, Sister said she would take all three of my children the next day. She told me where I could get their uniforms from. There was a nursery school as well, so they could take Mia. She gave me a guided tour of the nursery classroom, it was open plan; you could see the pride she had in her school. It was very modern and there were parents who helped with reading classes. They also did French from nursery age, I thought this was very progressive. She was head of the infants and nursery school. She then introduced me to the headmaster of the primary school where Louise would go. He agreed to accept Louise. I bought the badges for their blazers from the school. I had to sew the school badge on.

I headed back to the school in Perivale. I went into my son's class and asked the teacher, who was very young, what had happened. She said when she turned around from writing on the board, Allen was on top of another boy, who sat directly behind him. She separated them and told Allen off. She mentioned it was very hard to control thirty something children of their age.

The mother of the child complained to the headmaster the following day and he sent for Allen. The headmaster asked Allen, "Why did you attack your classmate?" He would not reply, confronted by two adults one a very angry mother.

I asked Allen where his coat was. He showed me. It was hanging on a hook with the other coats. I put his coat on him and told the teacher, "I am removing him from this school." I then went to the nursery and picked up Mia. My children did a lot of walking that day, as I went to Louise's school and spoke to her headmistress. I told her I wanted all three children in the same school. I thanked her for her interest in my daughter and I left with Louise, Allen and Mia.

We got the bus to Wembley and then on to the shop where they sold the school uniform. I fitted them out with the list given to me by the nun. They looked very smart when they were fitted.

I put the bill on my credit card. I had one, but did not use it very much and always paid it in full. This was the most I ever put on the card, needs must. I chatted with the children excitedly, telling them about, their new school and that they would love it.

That evening when I was putting Allen to bed, I asked him, "What happened at school?" He said, "The boy kept stabbing me in the back with a pencil and he would not stop. I told him to stop, but he would not listen to me." I told my son, "If someone beats you unfairly you have my permission to fight back and take your punishment that is if you have to. Do not worry about wetting the bed. I have a washing machine downstairs and plenty of sheets. I have put a rubber sheet to protect the mattress." He never wet the bed again. As I tucked him in I said, "Do not be afraid to tell the teacher if something like that happens again. You will be going to a new school in the morning. It looks a lovely school." I spent the rest of the night stitching three badges on their blazers.

I always loved their new school. It was a good school with a family atmosphere, it was the nearest I could get to private education. I loved the school plays. I welled up every time I saw one of my children on the stage in Christmas plays. Summer fairs and all school events I enjoyed. I was sorry when my youngest daughter Mia finished primary school and moved on to a secondary school...

Chapter 59

A Christmas Remembered

It was John's custom on a Christmas morning to visit his family with the children. A few days before Christmas we were invited to visit my younger sister at her flat in London. It was a great night, she plied me with a cocktail of, one part vodka, two parts dry Martini, ice and lemon. It was delicious and intoxicating.

There was stimulating conversation I could be corrected on that point. It is my custom to talk on all subjects under the sun when I have being plied with the correct lubricant.

The time passed in a haze and soon it was the early hours of the morning when we left for home. As we walked through the court yard on the way to the car, I thought I was sober but moon walking. Each step took a long time to reach the ground, my three children and husband were unaware of my condition. The children were tired, asleep or sleepy and my husband was driving.

I have to add that I did not drink much in those days; however the name cocktail seemed very sophisticated and exciting to me. I never had one before.

I was also on a high as I loved being with my family, it brought back memories of home and St Stephen's Day at Pery House.

St Stephens's Day, a happy day, a party at the maiden aunt's in Pery Square. Necks scrubbed, hair washed, gleaming with health, ribbons ornate, shiny faces, we made our way in relays. My father was first with the older children, out the door before they had time to look a mess. My mother followed on with the younger ones.

The door to Pery House was large, green and shiny, the knocker ornate. It gleamed like gold. My hand went in the letter box to find a key, dangling upon a string. Daddy opened the door wide. The hall was well lit, large and square. Aunts appeared from every door. With hugs and kisses we were ushered into the back sitting room, Aunts helped remove hats and coats. We were welcomed in to see the crib and say a prayer. The crib, a barn was lit, with red lights, the rays came through a little window at the side. A tableau told the story of kings and shepherds, parents and a baby in a manger.

Then to the dining hall to pay homage to the aunts and uncles' wives, 'how big you have grown. What class are you in now'? Around the fire the gathering of the clan with aunts and sisters-in-law all seated in honoured places. Broadly smiling. Sherry in hand with pleasantries complete, they called their off springs, one by one, to do a turn, a song, a poem, an Irish dance. The pride shone through the mammies' eyes when their young one excelled. When my turn came I froze remembering none. My Mammy eyed me sternly. They settled for 'I am a little Tea Pot' with actions, I was a little old for that one. All were content, loud clapping; I escaped for yet another year.

I stood in the back hall, looked up through a circular wide staircase, four flights to the ceiling. It was so high, dim and scary. Cousins played hide and seek in the dark shadows of the stairs, hiding in nooks and crannies, sliding on the banisters... Laughing when an aunt called "Come down from there, you will hurt yourself" and "What are you doing up there?"

At last the call to supper came and to the kitchen we descended. The door unlocked, the ceilings high, the kitchen came to life, a table laid to our delight. Enormous kettles boiling; pot with pudding bubbling on the Aga; moulded jellies quivering in all the colours of the rainbow; homemade soda breads of brown and white, spotted dog; silver salted beef, ham and turkey; tomatoes, salad and beetroot; bottles of lemonade and orange; pots of tea; hot plum pudding with ice cream and custard. The crowning glory was the cake, a snowy mountain with Christmas trees of green, sledges with little boys and girls, mirror pools for skaters encrusted in a cloud of silver beads.

The supper downed with much delight and compliments to aunties flew about. Then sleepy children helped with hats and coats, then homeward bound. They were given hugs, kisses and waves from the aunts, on the steps of Pery House. To dream of feasts fit for a king and of the good and kind devoted aunts of Pery Square.

So to move on to this Christmas Day. I was busy in the kitchen with the turkey bread sauce, gravy, Brussels, carrots, parsnips and the most important, roast potatoes.

My husband and the children went to visit my husband's niece and his cousins to wish them a happy and joyful Christmas. I was happy to be left in peace to make the final preparations for the Christmas dinner. I thought I would re-create my sister's cocktails, so I made one or maybe two. In the meantime, I peeled potatoes and placed them in boiling water, supposedly for five minutes. The plan was to roast them after they were parboiled.

Time flew by as I turned on the TV, salty tears dropping into my cocktail as I watched Santa visit little children in hospital over Christmas.

My family arrived back home, I checked my potatoes on the stove to find they were creamed, swimming in boiling water. That is how we had mashed potatoes on Christmas Day. not by design but by default.

Chapter 60

Flower Power

On a hot summer's day we went to Hyde Park to walk around the Serpentine, the lake is in the middle of Hyde Park. If you could not go to the seaside, or visit the country's green and pleasant land, on a summer's day, it was the next best thing to do.

John would not want to go, he would complain about the lack of parking. In the end he would agree and after a little difficulty, we would find a parking spot. Our little party headed off on this Sunday afternoon to walk along by Hyde Park's railings and marvel at the artists' work on display. Then, to stand a while and listen to the speakers at Hyde Park Corner.

This was the time of flower power, the flower power movement was a passive resistance, non-violence towards government policy, the war in Vietnam for example. Mahatma Gandhi's movement in his own country was opposed to violent revolution and he led the passive resistance, non-violent protest, in their fight for independence on 15th August 1947.

Flower power reached its climax at the Woodstock music festival of 1969 and went on into the late Sixties and early Seventies.

As we entered the park we were greeted by the beautiful people: young men in bell bottomed colourful trousers and flowery shirts, women with flowers in their hair, dressed in long flowing dresses of cheese cloth and tie died cotton, in rainbow colours, skirts in Indian earth-coloured greens and oranges. A girl with curly red hair handed me a flower chanting their mantra "Peace and love." "Peace and love." One felt for a moment in time it was possible. We moved on to the river Serpentine and the lake, sat in the restaurant overlooking the water, with a coffee, in a shady area and enjoyed watching the families and couples rowing on the lake in their boats and the duck feathers of lapis lazuli and emerald green. People were leisurely enjoying the moment, promenading around the path by the lake.

Chapter 61

Depression

O n the occasion when I had finished a conversation that was going around in circles with June about Robin, I felt I was surrounded in negativity. I was worried about June's comment about the Black Arts; I spend hours dissecting the meaning of his symptoms. The nuns in the convent school I went to told us that it was a sin to believe in the Black Arts. She told us about how it was, in the old days, in the country, if a cow stopped giving milk, it was said that a neighbour was envious and put a spell on their neighbour's cow. It caused a lot of anger between neighbours.

Perhaps, I let my mind run on with thoughts of this subject matter. I reasoned that Black Arts existed in Ireland in the old days. I dismissed this thought. My Daddy told us a story, one winter's night, about a woman who came back to Ennis from England, after her father died. She missed him so much she called him back from the other side. She had a ouija board and called him up. The old man sat by the fire and would not go back. Daddy said it was Old Nick himself. We Irish love a good ghost story. Sometimes our imagination can take over as I recall very clearly.

There was no television in Limerick when I was a child; the cinema was for a special occasion. Daddy or Mammy would read out an interesting snippet of news from the paper or magazine, Daddy's favourite poems and sometimes my father read us a book.

After school it was our custom to have a cup of tea and sit by the fire seeking comfort on cold, rainy days. Mammy was reading a story, about a nanny in a large country house, caring for two orphaned children, who were possessed by bad spirits. We begged her to read it to us. When you sit by the fire, looking into the embers in a dreamlike state, the story takes on a life of its own.

There was a part lodged in my memory, when the nanny was in the children's room, a face came to the window closer and closer until the face as white as death, pressed against the window pane. The book was made into a film in black and white. It still scared me years later.

Soon after this time my mother developed a lump on her throat, she was convinced that it was cancer and cried many tears wondering what would become of her children when she was no longer there to care for them. I consoled her as best I could, while being very worried on her behalf.

My aunt visited us every day after her siesta occasionally Mammy and my aunt had words over a small matter, this time my brother got involved. It was unheard of for one of the children to say a word against my aunt. Mammy and my aunt were very close, they were identical twins. Having words came and went like the wind.

Mammy went to hospital when the lump burst but it was only a cyst after all. That night my aunt and mother were sitting by the fire chatting, the best of friends.

I went to the kitchen to make a pot of tea for them... I felt some one was watching me. The hairs stood up on the back of my neck. I looked out of the window.

I saw a pale face floating in the darkness coming towards me. Logic told me it was a sheet flying in the wind, if I kept looking, it would disappear. The face came closer and closer. The words of the story Mammy read went through my subconscious. The face kept coming it pressed up against the window pane, then he called my name.

I went into shock, clung to the wall of the dining room. I could not speak. I could not call to get my Mammy's or my aunt's attention. I banged my fist against the wall. My mouth opened wide but no sound came out. Mammy and my aunt shot out of their chairs and grabbed me; my aunt said that I had received an electrical shock from the kettle.

Mammy had that knowing look and went out in the back yard where she found my brother. He was trying to get my attention, get a cup of tea and a biscuit; out the kitchen window.

He did not want to face my Aunt. Mammy gave him a clip around the ear for frightening me and sent him to his room.

I was put to bed given a cup of hot sweet tea and told to drink it up as it was good for shock, next morning there was no mention of this incident. Life went on.

When I thought of Robin's ill-health, I found no answer. Women seem to think they have to be superwoman and cure all ills; I was powerless and could do nothing about it.

The stress of my life at home was getting to me so I went to see my doctor. My throat was tight and I constantly suffered with stress and anxiety. My doctor put me on Valium. I continued working, studying, living day to day. When I visited my doctor he had a very full surgery and just wrote the prescription. Over time I got used to the dosage it was not working. I told the doctor how I felt. He increased my dosage.

In times of hardship and loneliness, in my mind, I would travel back to a happier time. I did not want to share with my children the freedom we had in Ireland in my youth. They were not always easy times but we were very creative in our games and street play. They would not understand, as I was so protective of them. Do not go with strangers, you cannot go on your own and so on. Now I feel safe to tell them about a picnic, that the children our street went on.

The word on the street was, Blackwater and a picnic on Bank Holiday Monday. My sister Phillis and neighbour Anthony were in charge. First, we had to get our mother's approval with discussions on who would be going and how. We put up strong arguments in favour of going; weather permitting a decision to go was not forthcoming until the morning. Many prayers were said that night for good weather. On the day the sun was shining! The question now was would Mammy let my younger brother Dermot go as she thought he was too young. A group of children stood looking over our wall. There were long negotiations. Anthony gave his assurance and the group said 'Let him go Mrs G… we will look after him.'

Our schoolbags were packed with a small bottle of milk, sugar, spam sandwiches and butter and jam sandwiches, Mariette biscuits and a bottle of lemonade purchased from the shop. Older children carried a kettle and we all had a cup.

We congregated outside our house with mothers at gates to wave us off and a word from my father, "When you are asking for permission to enter the woods, tell the man in charge who your father is." That seemed to cover it all.

At long last we started our adventure, Anthony and Phillis leading the way.

We passed Mrs Windrums and Mrs Long's smiling faces. They were happy to see such a happy and hopeful group. We headed out on the road towards Hassetts Cross through Ballanty and out in the open countryside to pick up the disused railway track at Parteen.

A younger member of our party wanted to eat one of his sandwiches, a group voice answered, 'not until you get there'. Our little legs got in stride with the tracks after a slow start. We broke into song and we were truly on our way. 'This old Man he played one.' 'You're in the Army now, not behind a plough' and many other marching songs.

After some time we arrived at Ardnacrusha Hydroelectric Plant and walked along the bank of the river Shannon in single file. The wide and deep waters made its way towards great turbines supplying electricity to the county. The occasional fish popped up his head to catch a morsel floating on the glistening water.

We climbed a stile and came upon the main road, walked down the hill passed Barry's shop and arrived at a gate to the wood and Blackwater.

We rang the bell and asked the forester if we could picnic in the wood. We let him know, who we were and that we were from Farranshone. He instructed us not to damage the young saplings and the dangers of fires were pointed out. We must put out the fire after the kettle was boiled. We all agreed. The gate was duly opened and we trooped through.

Our first steps into the wood were magical; surrounded with a canopy of different shades of green with the sunlight filtering through; the smells of the earth were tropical and moist from the morning mist, birds calling and answered from the green canopy echoing one side of the forest to the other. The rippling sounds of the black water sparkling as it rolled over pebbles in the midday sun.

Trees from ancient times, all shapes and sizes welcomed us, with their gnarled and friendly bark. To climb, to sit, for us to hug, to shade and shelter, under branches. Young saplings, promising a future forest, a new tomorrow.

We had entered a land of beauty and adventure. The girls' Area was the Dell, a hollow surrounded by trees. The boys, the island, our instructions were not to go on the island as it was the boys' domain.

Anthony told us if we put a match into the kettle, the tea would not be smoky, he then showed us where in the stream to put our lemonade packed tightly between stones to keep cool and we were left to our own devices.

We set about making a fire, surrounding it with stones to rest the kettle on. The tea was served; it was the greatest cup of tea and picnic ever.

The day was ours to explore, wander and play, the forest floor our domain, sounds abounded with laughter, names rang out through the woods as we played games, screams were heard as we caught our friends in hide and seek.

The boys swam in a natural pool of deep dark water, doing acrobatic dives from high places, while we watched from the other side of the bank. A large old tree had fallen to the centre of the pool; the boys ran along it and dived into the depths of the pool.

Dermot walked along the tree, freckles and golden hair gleaming in the sun; I froze as he positioned himself for a dive and in he went. Screams of horror went out, the big boys dived in and hauled him out, there was hysterical laughter he was a hero of the day. It was put to him that he had to learn to swim first.

All was well. The sun was going down as we made our way back with our memories of a never to be forgotten picnic. Anxious mothers looked up Farranshone road for our return and there were calls from neighbours, "Are they back yet?"

Chapter 62

Robin Goes Home

The children were growing up very quickly. Glacier Metal kept Robin employed as long as they possibly could. They sent a letter to June to come and see them. They had to let him go. He was not getting better.

He had started getting seizures. I would be uneasy; a bad feeling would come over me. Then I would hear June scream and I would run up the stairs to help her with Robin. I suggested to her that I would take him to the doctors. She agreed. On the way there he said to me, "I used to be a teacher; I do not know what is wrong with me." I went in to the examination room with him. I explained his problem as best I could. The doctor decided to send him to the hospital where he stayed for two weeks. The hospital doctors told June that they would send a report to his doctor. I went to see him and see what could be done for him and what the diagnosis was. The doctor told me there was nothing they could do for him.

They had given him series of tests. The doctor did not give me a name for his illness. I did not know enough to ask the question, I accepted his diagnosis. I told June they did not find out what was wrong and they could not do anything for him. June accepted this as it coincided with her beliefs regarding his illness.

June and Robin had a friend who visited them on occasions. He told them that Robin's mother knew someone who could cure him. He was going to Grenada on holidays and Robin could travel with him home to his mother. I told the doctor what was decided. He said, "Do what you feel will help him, we can do nothing more."

June wrote to his mom and told her she would be sending him home. It was a sad day when he left. He was thirty-four. June thought it was in his best interests, he may get better with the sunshine and returning to his mom and Grenada. That would have been our wish, though I did not hold out much hope. On the day before he was due to travel, June sent him to a barber's shop. It was a little way from our house, but he had to have a haircut. He was gone a long time. We went out on the road to look for him but could not find him.

A friend met him and returned with him. He had a black eye. We never knew what happened to him and he did not remember. We thought he went into the wrong house and someone got angry with him when he tried to enter. June still did not realised how far he progressed with his illness. Now I realise he needed constant supervision. Robin died in Grenada aged 38 with Alzheimer's. In later years both of his daughters Joan and Ester died also of Alzheimer's in their mid to late thirties.

Chapter 63

June And Girls Go Home

On the Saturday, we went to visit family and we were back late. June opened her bedroom door slightly and called me. Her eyes looked wild. She was so scared she said she saw an item of Robin's clothes on the floor in the bathroom. There was no way it should be there. I reassured her that there was nothing to worry about. I talked to her for a while. I realised she was having a breakdown. The following day she took to her bed, getting worse. Joan came to me and said Mommy is not well, she wants to see you. She was lying in her bed, saying she was going to die. She wanted Joan and Ester to come and lie on the bed with her for the last time. She was calling them to come to her. They were scared as this behaviour was so out of character for June.

In all the years we lived as family in one house we never had a cross word. I was getting scared for her and the children. I did not think. I just said to her, "Get up out of that bed and feed your children! They are hungry." It was the only thing I could think of to say. I look back in hindsight and see I did the best I could, given my age and experience. I now know more about depression as I suffered with it. My depression got worse after they left.

She was suffering the loss of her husband; it was like a death in her family. She wanted to grieve for her loss. When you live under such pressure, for so long and it is removed, you do not know what to do next. You are lost and alone and do not know where to turn.

She got out of her bed and came downstairs; she got her purse and gave Joan money to go to the shop for eggs and beans. I went with Joan. I wanted to chat with her and let her know that her Mommy would be fine. She was just upset.

June was very quiet in the kitchen when we came back. I knew she was not happy with me. She just wanted to give up. I would not let her. I would have fed her and the children but that would not have got her on her feet. In the kitchen, she was boiling potatoes. She sat the children down to a nice hot meal of mashed potatoes, eggs and beans.

She got dressed and went out on the road with the children. The next day she told me that she had decided to go home to Trinidad. She had booked her flight and would go as soon as she had sorted her affairs. She needed the support of her parents and family to help her get through this time. I accepted what she said and did not try to change her mind. She went some weeks later after shipping her goods to Trinidad.

Some years later she told me she did not have the money to take her goods out of customs in Trinidad when the ship landed. Her loss was great as it was all her possessions, gathered from her years in the UK. such as mementoes, utensils and clothes.

She seemed to improve with the thought that she was going home. Her family had a very nice house near the university in Trinidad. I heard that she had a breakdown when she was safely in her father's house. She recovered and got an office job in a large store in Trinidad.

When she left I missed her, Joan and Ester, but I did not know how I felt as I was also depressed. If I kept on my feet I would not give in. I resolved never to have tenants again even if I had to work all the hours God sent me.

Chapter 64

End It All

When you have no dream to dream and you are left with a feeling of nothingness, that is when you cannot visualise a future. You are depressed. Who can say why or how you get depressed? Who can explain it? If you knew how it happened you could put it right, it is like a drop of water on a stone, from the time of your birth, every hurt, building up and wearing you down, smaller and smaller, until you vanish. That is where you turn to the wall. Now I had convinced myself that the world would be a better place without me. I had slowly got more and more depressed. The doctor changed my medication to a stronger tablet. I wanted to escape and run away. I told my doctor that I had very bad feelings. I did not care if I lived or died. When I was crossing the road a bus nearly knocked me down, I was so sorry it did not, I felt I was a burden to my family and my children.

My husband was very capable and a good father. The family would survive much better without me. My children would grow and develop under his care. In those days there was no diagnosis for post-natal depression, after baby blues. The fire that happened at home, when I was in hospital giving birth to my last child, played on my mind; the years of watching Robin grow worse with Alzheimer's; living out of a suitcase, moving from room to room before we got a house. Life's struggle took its toll. I had taken extra tablets to sleep at night and to get through the day. I was very unhappy. I digress simply to share with you a time that I had a sinking feeling not unlike the feeling I had on a daily basis. This was when I was a teenager before I left home.

It was a bright sunny day with a chill wind, when you were in the shade and I decided to go with my friend to Ardanacrusha, to a place they called the culvert. There was a tunnel where the overflow from the river Blackwater came into the pool. It was alongside the river Shannon and a favourite place to swim. We cycled out about five miles from Limerick City. After a walk along the banks of the Shannon at Ardanacrusha we made our way with our bikes to the culvert. My friend sat sunning herself on the grass verge near the water, looking for a sun tan. Not much of a chance of that in Ireland; the best to hope for, was to burn red. I went in for a swim. The water was cold and when I got to the centre of the pool I pulled myself up on a wide pole, protruding out of the water. I sat on it and tried to get warm with the sunshine. After some time, I had to leave my sunny spot, lowered myself into the icy water and swam back. I sank down like a lead weight; the water covered my head, sending me into a state of shock. I gulped water, down and down I went. I realised I was drowning and nobody was watching from the grassy verge. I struggled to raise myself up. My eyes opened looking at the dark cloudy water laced with grass and after what seemed an eternity, I started to ascend slowly, terror engulfing me in every pore of my being. At last I arrived at the surface. I swam to the verge and looked around. People were chatting, sleeping, reading and no one was aware. I had nearly drowned, while they got on with living their lives, in peaceful, beautiful surroundings. I did not tell my friend who was reading a book. She looked at me and asked if I was OK. I said the water was very cold. I did not swim for the rest of the summer after that incident and from then on I had a great respect for the dangers of perilous waters.

I continued to work, came home and worked again. After several overdoses, which I recovered from, I would go to work the next day and worked all day. One night I took a serious overdose. I had regained consciousness the next morning and asked my daughter to get the doctor. I deeply regretted putting my children through such a stressful time and have to live with that memory. When the doctor came I had a seizure and was taken to the heart ward at the local hospital. When I came to, in the middle of the night, I could not sleep. I went out of the ward to a dismal corridor, dimly lit and sat on a bench. I looked down the long corridor and saw a nurse approaching from the other end: a dot on the horizon. As she made her way up the hall, she got larger as she came closer. She sat on my bench and started to chat. She said, "A young woman tried to kill herself today. She is in that ward. Everybody in the ward is fighting to live." I said, "That was me." She disappeared very quickly.

As you slip deeper into depression, it is like travelling down a long tunnel blinkered. You become more isolated and lonely. You grow inward; you do not see a solution. Depression is not a recognisable illness, like cancer, or a broken arm, that can be seen. Depression is an all-consuming deep pit. It eats away at your soul, crushes you in ways you cannot dream of, destroys your health and wellbeing and leads you along paths you would not travel. You go so low you cannot see the road that leads you home. Your confidence is squashed; you are in the sludge and mire. Where is the path that leads you home? You are in your own hell and stay longer than you should. Where did you go wrong? How did you get there? Did you expect too much of yourself and loved ones? You cannot accept failings at any level; even in yourself. It is in your hands to change. Is it that easy to change the tracks in your brain? Retrain the brain, set down new pathways, focus on new activities, move on to find another path, change the channel, come out the other side and once again join the human race.

I was in the heart ward and they pumped out my stomach. I do not know what else they did to revive me. I do not remember coming home from the hospital. Before I left, the doctor told me to drink a small glass of soda water in milk, a little but often to reline my stomach.

During the morning, I was lying awake in my bed and there was a man sitting beside my bed. I was surrounded by an overpowering feeling of love. It was not of this world. I looked at him and thought, is he my grandfather, or a doctor. He was definitely a man of authority. I did not speak. He spoke to my mind. He said, 'This is the last time I can pull you through.' I knew in a split-second. I no longer had a fear of death. This man would come for me when the time was right, he would help me to cross over. I got a second chance. I do not have a fear of death to this day. I was not aware that I had a fear of death.

I never took an antidepressant again. I visited my doctor, he would not prescribe antidepressants for me and I did not ask him to. I went through a very bad time with withdrawal symptoms. They lasted about two years; I was not right for many years. I could not believe the energy I had. I cleaned all the kitchen cupboards and relined them. The tablets must have been slowing me down. I slowly came out of the depression. I worked, I studied and took pleasure in little things again. My children, whom I loved, filled my life with day to day living. Every achievement that they gained were great joys to John and I. I learned to get on with my life and live for another day.

I came out of a downward trend. I cannot say why, what happened, who helped. I believe it was the man beside my bed. . I saw the bottom. Now I was moving slowly upward step by step, nothing fast you understand slowly, slowly, I cleaned my house. I put on Christmas music, lit a scented candle, put fairy lights on a small tree, watched all the Christmas movies on TV and now I looked forward to family visits over the Christmas season. I was still floating between depression and optimism, a marginal line: ballet shoes on a tightrope.

Chapter 65

Daddy's Sister Clare

Aunty Clare was deeply religious and would have been a nun except for having had TB as a child. I had been told that a convent would not have her as they regarded her as being delicate. Life was very hard in some of the convents. My aunt contracted the disease when she was very young. She walked with a slight limp but she did not allow it to stop her from doing work for the Catholic Church.

Daddy once told me that when she was in a hospital on a TB ward, she was the only child on the ward. She witnessed many of the other patients dying. Nursing nuns ran the ward and there would have being a lot of prayers said, for the patent, when they died. When my aunt eventually left, cured, from the hospital, she played funerals with her dolls. Her family were horrified and cried many tears for her.

Aunty Clare was my godmother, she felt that my religious welfare was her responsibility; she had a challenge on her hands. She tried to get me involved in various Catholic organisations; I tried some and very gently faded out. She would then try something else. She was a good woman and she did not force me. When I made my confirmation she gave me a beautiful doll, with a whole wardrobe of lovely clothes for the doll, a cape of red velvet, lined with purple silk and many very beautiful dresses.

She was a gifted dressmaker. She and her sister had learned their trade from their aunts. When a large family had many girls and they did not marry, dressmaking was a genteel skill, as you did not have to go out to work. My father remembered the side saddles hanging over the banisters, so the Ladies of the Hunt, could have a fitting.

Aunty Clare visits me in England and on one occasion I told my son, 'My aunt is coming to stay for a few days. You will have to vacate your room.' He got very cross which was unusual for him. I ignored it and went to prepare the room for my aunt. My son had locked his bedroom door, which was very odd. I was cross and ordered him to open it at once. The room was messy, nothing unusual in that...I did notice the clothes that were supposed to be in the drawers, were at the end of the wardrobe, so I put them in the wash. I was tired but busy hoovering and cleaning. He was hanging around the hall in my shadow.

My aunty came, stayed three days and I took her to the airport. I came back to organise the room for my son. I pulled out the drawer, saw a long tail and in a reflex action I pulled open the second drawer to see a large gerbil that looked like a rat. I fled the room and the house, sat in the garage at the back of the garden and cried until the children came home from school. They called for me and I answered from the garage. John came at the same time and my daughter Louise told him where I was. My son was told to remove the gerbil from the house in no uncertain terms.

I then remembered that he had asked if he could have one from the school lab. They were breaking up for the summer holiday and the gerbils could not be left in the classroom. I had a terror of mice, when I first came to England and lived in very poor housing.

My fear of mice started in the Grove. When John was working nights, I was on my own. The gas cooker was in the room where the food was cooked and the bucket where waste products had been was also in the room with the food press holding sugar, flour, butter, etc. There was no fridge. After dark the mice would run around the bin and the gas cooker, while I knitted layettes for my baby. I would not scream, there was no point. I was afraid that the mice would come on my bed when I slept. I slept fitfully waking and sitting up looking around to make sure they were not there, that they had not got under the candlewick bedspread, I would shake the bed clothes to make absolutely sure. I lived with a deeply buried fear that came out years later, when I saw a field mouse near a little shed in my garden. I went into hysterics. John dismantled the shed and burnt all the wood in a bonfire. I had not thought about mice when John was on days or in the morning. The nights were long and isolated for me. The trauma of my living conditions remains hidden, in the innermost part of my brain, only to emerge in a hysterical outburst, when triggered by the sight of a mouse. I told Allen absolutely no he could not have one. My poor aunt never knew and slept for three days in the room, keeping company with a gerbil.

I was with my aunt when she died. I travelled to Ireland and stayed the night and slept in her room. I thought she had gone during the night. She stopped breathing and then started breathing very quietly. I think she did not want to frighten me so she waited until morning. In the morning I put my shuttle bed under her bed. I went to the bathroom and tidied up. I sat with her. I said in my mind, 'Please God, take her, she has worked very hard for you in her lifetime, let her go now.' She went. I have a feeling that I was angry at the time I said it, she had suffered so much. I had remembered her walking on a Sunday afternoon delivering holy books in the rain and cold. She has earned her place with the Lord.

Chapter 66

Brighton

Our first seaside holiday was to Brighton. We all needed a holiday. I did not know if I could get through the next winter, if I did not have a holiday.

I usually went to Ireland because one of my parents was ill or for a funeral or wedding. I would travel by the train and boat always arriving back in England having caught a heavy cold. These times held memories of a winter's travel, bidding farewell in the station, large and dome-like, clinically clean. Cream tiles with loneliness lingered in every pore. Birds, flying high, were coming home to roost, to nest under the eaves. Families grouped together, like midgets around the carriage door, filling in the silent moments with meaningless chit-chat. A whistle signalling the train moving slowly outward bound. A last look back, to my little family group, disappearing into the distance and I am gone.

I decided we would pack our case and head off on the train to Brighton. There was no booking made. I told John and the children that we would put our suitcases into storage for left luggage, at the train station and head off to see if we could get a hotel to stay in. If we did not get a place, we would collect our cases when we were leaving Brighton, on our way back to London. We would have a great day by the sea.

There was a worry; the landlord would not accommodate us, as we were a mixed race couple. This fear was left over from the days of looking for rooms to rent. I also had not a great deal of money. Credit cards were not an option for me. I paid as I went. A credit card was for a real emergency, not a holiday. To use a credit card would mean paying it off, from money to pay household bills.

As we rounded the corner facing the blue sea and golden sand, there was a pub next to us with a sign marked "vacancies" on a noticeboard, in we went the children had a lemonade and

John had a drink. I chatted to the landlady and asked her if she had any vacancies. She said when we had finished our drinks to come and see her. She gave us a large family room with two beds and a camp bed. I asked her how much a night. She said £5. I quickly calculated that we could do five nights which meant six days. She agreed and I handed over the money. John collected our case from the station and we were ready to take to the beach.

John bought ice creams and went for a walk with the children, while I settled down to a good book, making myself comfortable in a deckchair on the beach. When he returned, we went to find a supermarket where we bought the making of sandwiches, buns and drinks and returned with them to the beach.

As evening approached we went back to our lodgings, showered, dressed to impress and headed out for our supper, which was egg, chips and beans. This pattern was repeated throughout the week with variations on the supper: sausage, egg, chips and beans. We changed one night to a different restaurant for fish, chips and mushy peas. As a celebration we went to an Indian restaurant, very posh with red flock paper on the walls and candles in little lampshades. We had dhal, curry and rice. We took long walks in the evenings along the promenade and then to bed.

It was the first holiday we had by the sea and we all looked the better for it and it gave me the confidence to be adventurous and try a different holiday next time.

Chapter 67

A Little About Me

April 1 I was busy preparing dinner. I was in and out of the dining room while a programme was on the TV. It was a three minute documentary about the cultivation of spaghetti called 'The Swiss spaghetti Harvest.' I had glimpses of women harvesting spaghetti from a tree. It was explained how each strand grew to the same length. As I said I was in and out of the kitchen. Our family were not spaghetti eaters in Ireland. It was a daily diet of potatoes and rice for pudding. I said to myself, 'Well I never knew that' and forgot about it. I did not see follow-up news stating that it was an April 1 Fool's Day hoax. Years later I was watching the greatest hoax carried out and there it was. Until then I had always thought spaghetti grew on trees. This programme was first aired by Richard Dibble on *Panorama* in 1957. I had not previously heard about it.

On a sunny day I came from work and went to the garden to unwind a little. Earlier that month John had planted some tomato plants. He told me that his father would not let him plant as he said, they would not grow. He always worked at a speed and I suppose the plants wanted to be placed into the earth and nurtured, to develop in a healthy way. I looked at the flowers and my eye was drawn towards the tomato plant; there proudly sat a large red tomato. I was amazed and rushed indoors to tell John the good news. John started to laugh and came out with me to see the tomato, which on closer inspection was tied with thread to the tree. It was not even April 1.

I am not telling you these tales to seem stupid, just that preoccupation with the daily tasks of life can override your absorption of other facts. It is good sometimes to laugh at yourself.

It is important here to analyse why I had such a difficult life when I first travelled. I was always one to follow my own path and I lived with the consequence even when I knew I would get into trouble. When I was young, living at home, I did not know there was more than one way to approach a subject; that you could be more diplomatic, put your point in some other way, not say your truth if it was not necessary and you could get your own way. I would accept a decision made against me, or argue the point, which would cause confrontation. I can make some decisions in a split-second. I would stay with that decision, even if it was not such a good decision, when there were better ways. I would work on the consequences of my decision to make it better.

I have a strong sense of what is morally correct. I have great trouble going against what I feel is my moral fibre. I will over analyse and worry about it. If I make a friend, they stay. The fact that other people think that they are unsuitable will not influence me. However I can be discerning in who I chose as a friend. Family and friends have found me difficult to deal with. I am a non-conformist. I do not run with the pack. My family motto is where I cannot find a path I will make one. Sometimes I have found myself isolated and alone. I do not seek out confrontation. I like the words of Desiderata (Avoid loud, aggressive persons; they are a vexation to the spirit). I would run from confrontation if I could. My problem is, I do not see it coming. Sometimes a person is in my face shouting at me and I have been unaware of their feeling. Autism comes to mind. I am unaware of the signs; I do not look for them. A thought will cross my mind that all is not well but my wish for peace and goodwill, even at my expense, will overrule my thoughts. I do not read people well. I do my work and focus on keeping the roof over my head. I have strived for a better education for my family and myself and their welfare and helping them to a better life.

At one of my work assessments, when I was the assistant accountant in a large company, my team always produced their work on time. My boss said I was rather stoic in my dealings with others; I was not sure what he meant. Did he think I was too serious? Life and responsibility had made me serious. I went to the book store and asked for any book they had on stoicism. They showed me a book (Letters Of A stoic} *Epistulea Morales*

Ad Lucilium by Seneca, iIt was written in the years BC62 to 65. Its content was, if you lost all your family by murder, rape and pillage you would plod along. In other words endurance and acceptance was the order of the day. Because that is what you did. I thought well OK, not perfect, but it helped me get through a difficult time in my life. I feel I could do better if I had that killer instinct but I lacked the will and stamina to go in for the kill, in business and life in general. I thought too much about the effect on others. I was afraid I would break down and lose my point, in standing up for myself, or I should have said no! More often, when it was called for. I tended to want to keep people happy. People think that I have free will. They are upset and surprised when I do not conform to their norm. I do not want them to conform to my norm. My youngest daughter put it very well. 'Mom may not choose the same path as you but she will get there in the end.'

When I look back on my life I think given the same set of circumstances, I would do the same again, with some minor adjustments that come with experience. I did not, all of a sudden wake up one morning with a stubborn streak and fierce independence.

Chapter 68

Uncle Steve

I recall a visit on a Sunday to my Uncle Steve. How I got invited to visit my Uncle Steve's family I do not know. One morning a girl came to pick me up and Mammy said I was to go with her to visit my Uncle Steve's house, so off I went. I may have been seven or eight at the time. My Uncle Steve's house was at the bottom of Farranshone across from Lanny Fraser's pub. The girl's name was Cathleen. She had red hair and was very kind to me. Uncle Steve Barry was a cousin of my mother's. His house was very dark, that is compared to our house. There were pictures on the wall, copies of paintings by the old Masters. One was a table set for a feast with fruit and a dead pheasant of many coloured feathers on the table. Another was of kittens, resembling a chocolate box screen in the Forties. Sitting by the fire was Uncle Steve's son. He never spoke or looked at me. I asked Mammy about him and was told he had a brain tumour. He later had an operation and died on the operating table. I could not say what age he was. I now think he was in his early Twenties. I was sad to think he was in pain. Mammy said, "He was in great pain so it was better God took him, if the doctors could not do anything to help him. It was God's will."

Cathleen brought me swimming to Corbally. I would not go in the water at that time as I could not swim. I remember we were in some little huts by the river. They resembled beach huts, only we were not by the sea. She changed into her swimsuit in the hut. One Sunday we met a group of young people on the jetty. One of them was a cousin of mine. He was a young man, whose name was Conor and his father was my father's brother. He may have owned the hut Cathleen changed in. He was getting his boat ready to row on the river Shannon. There is a long history of rowers in our family as his father, my Daddy and brothers rowed, my cousins and now my nephews rowed in the world championship races. They have gold and silver medals and one rowed in the Olympics for Ireland twice. When they were young, they all belonged to one of Limerick's boat clubs either the Athlunkard Boat Club or St Michael's Boat Club.

My cousin said to Cathleen, "Would you like a trip up the river in my boat?". Somewhere in my mind I believe Cathleen said, "No, but Marie would like to go, wouldn't you Marie?" I had never been in a boat before, I did not know what to expect. I bravely stepped into the boat and he pushed away from the riverbank and started to row up the Shannon, where the water was calm and clear. I put my hand in the water and the water filtered through my fingertips. I saw the swans on the river and the beautiful scenery as he rowed along the river Shannon; all was well until we came towards Ardanacrusha power station. The enormous turbines were directly in front of us and I started to get stressed. I felt we would be sucked into the turbines. I was shy and afraid to say "please take me back" or cry as I did not want to appear a baby. He picked up that I was very uneasy and said, "We are safe here, I will not go any further. Do not worry, I will turn back just now." I knew he was trying to reassure me that we were safe and he would go no further. He stopped rowing and we bobbed up and down on the river, the turbines seemed to be drawing so near and I was panic-stricken. I was terrified of the roaring sound of the water going through the turbines. I was not happy until he turned back towards Cathleen and my feet were firmly on safe solid ground.

Cathleen then brought me home. When we got to the top of the road, where we would go down to her house or up to my house, she said, "Who do you like the best in our house?" That was a big question as I did not remember saying more than two words to her all day, please and thank you. She was a big girl and I was not so big. I went through her whole family. I said to her "I like your sister, Mary." She asked, "Who next?" I said, "I like Uncle Steve." "Who next?" "Aunty." "Who next?"Stephen." She said, "Don't you like me?" I said, "Yes." She was the last on my list. I do not know why I did it, I felt she should not ask. I would be trying to curry favour, if I said I liked her best, I may have been autistic in a way I felt I could not lie or was I just stubborn? She then said to me, "You can go home on your own now." The arrangements were that I had tea at her house. Her Mammy was expecting us.

As I started to walk in the direction of my house she would call me back. When she went through this ritual the next Sunday, I gave exactly the same answers; I knew she would call me back. She was a girl with a big personality and a good heart. I think she enjoyed the fact that I would not pander to her. I was a little in awe of her. She entered the Salesian Order and became a nun, some years later and I now feel I was sent to try her patience. She was put to the test by God. She passed with flying colours, as she collected me from our house again the following Sunday. She never showed that she resented me for not liking her best. She seemed to have forgotten until the end of the day.

I would have known Uncle Steve from when he passed our gate on his way to and from work. If I was with Mammy in our garden, Mammy would say, "Hello, Uncle Steve," He would touch his cap in recognition and respect, he did not say much. I got to know Uncle Steve better when I went to school. I came out the gate of the Salesian Convent at 12.30pm to go home for lunch he would be just passing the gate of our school at that moment, we all came out in our school uniforms, looking very smart in our school hats and navy gabardine coats in winter and our blue dresses with white collar and navy cardigans in summer. Uncle Steve would have his dirty working clothes on, as he was a fitter for the gas board. I would walk to my house with him. His chest was bad; more than likely from the gas where he worked. He would cough and spit on the road. I would cringe and hope no one in my class could see him. I could have avoided him quite easily, by hanging back a little and letting him go. I sought him out. I could not live with myself if I did not, he was family. He belonged to Mammy's family and therefore me. He would say to me "How are you Gandhi?" I would say, "Fine, Uncle Steve." We would walk the rest of the way in silence, as no words were necessary.

I asked my Mammy, "Why does Uncle Steve call me Gandhi?" She said, "When you were a baby you were small, very tanned from the sun with big brown eyes and you were very blond. Your hair took a long time to grow and I used to sit you in the pram outside our door. He would have seen you when he passed on his way to work."

There was a great love for Gandhi in Ireland as he believed in home rule and self-sufficiency for India and Eamon De Valera believed in home rule and self-sufficiency for Ireland. He was well known by our president at the time of his visit. He would have been in the newspaper and the news. Uncle Steve would have known about him, when he visited England because it was well publicised. One could think that Uncle Steve could see into the future, my husband was Indian and my family are Londoners of Asian descent.

Chapter 69

House Blessing

I answered a ring at the door and there was my parish priest. I was a little taken aback. He told me that my husband had paid him a visit and asked him to bless the house. I was very surprised as John did not go to church unless it was a baptism, communion, confirmation, funeral and at Christmas to stand at the back of the church during the Christmas Mass. He had not mentioned he was going to see the priest, or had been. I had not thought of it myself.

Father asked where the children were. I called them in from their play. We stood in the sitting room. The priest asked us to say the Lord's Prayer. He gave a short blessing, sprinkled holy water on us and the house was blessed. The priest was gone. I do not remember asking him if he would like a cup of tea and a biscuit, which would have been expected. I was still amazed that John had called him.

I went about my housework and the children resumed their play. I did not ask John why he asked the priest to bless the house. I knew a lot of grief and unhappiness had happened, since we moved into the house. I was happy he thought it would help. I have always believed that this small action cleansed our home. Melancholy and lingering sadness is a kind of sadness that floats in the background and tightens your throat, seeps into and lingers in the walls of the house.

The next few years moved on and life got better. We made friends outside of the family, entertained and were entertained. I was happy to get on with the rest of my life and watch my children grow into bright and intelligent children who did well in school and in life.

Chapter 70

My Journey

I have now journeyed through my early life, from the age of seventeen, as an emigrant to the UK and dipped into memories of my earlier days in Ireland. I hope you have enjoyed the journey with me. I had difficulty making a start on my story. Recalling the early years was a struggle and not always a happy time. I have tried to show the contrast between youth and adulthood, between the harsh realities of an emigrant, contrasting with the innocence of my youth in Ireland. We have now shared my journey on a rocky road with some smooth passages.

I was worried about opening Pandora's Box. Once I lifted the lid, it was therapeutic. I have greatly enjoyed recounting the stories of my youth and got lost in the memories. One has to remember, with memories, I have lived and seen, any group of people living, sharing with me at that time, would view it differently, as it would be seen through their eyes, they would walk through, changed by their experiences, in a different way. This is my story seen through my eyes, my mistakes and my decisions; I am proud of the good decisions and tried to make good, bad decisions. Take it as it is, do not read too much into it, life moves on and change happens. It was a growing time in my life, I got through and I am stronger as a result of it.

I have a family I love and I am very proud of the achievements that we gained. Emigration is a challenge for all, no matter what the reason. In our case it was made more difficult with prejudice and being a racially inter-married couple. To have the benefit of living with more than one culture, widens your understanding of mankind and educates you in the ways of the world. People are the same all over the world. They have the same wants and needs, a roof over their heads, work, food, education for their children, respect in their community and a peaceful world.

The experience of emigrants is still very relevant in today's society. With the movement of people across the world, due to the hardship of war, poverty and joining the European Community, jobs, housing and just surviving day by day for emigrants will be a struggle, until one day they will raise their heads and life will be normal and hopefully good. The influx of emigrants seeking asylum, if they are successful, will have their own problems to face. All immigrants are not poor; some have enormous wealth, skills, education. They may start at the bottom but will find their own level in society. One thinks of emigrants as being the poorest of the poor and clogging up the social services, this is not always the case. Immigration can put a drain on resources when dealing with the initial influx. They will however contribute to the progress and the development, both financially and culturally of any country. The need of first generation emigrants to succeed is very strong. Their ambition to succeed is passed down to the second third and fourth generations. This need to succeed will enhance all levels of society and will help to build a strong country and nation.

To emigrate in peaceful times, one is leaving a safe known environment, for the unknown. To emigrate in times of war is running in fear, to a safe environment and grasping at the unknown. The benefits can be worth the struggle. To be scared can place you in a position, that you challenge and stretch yourself, because you have no choice. I have enjoyed telling you my story. John and I were pioneers of our time, searching out new beginnings, in a new country. A new tribe in the making.

"If you cannot get rid of the family skeleton, you may as well make it dance."

George Bernard Shaw